ANCIENT SECRET
of the
FOUNTAIN OF YOUTH
COOKBOOK

Simple, Delicious Recipes
for Health & Longevity

Devanando Otfried Weise
Jenny Frederiksen

HARBOR PRESS

IMPORTANT NOTICE:

English Translation by
Ursula Zilinsky and Lisa Scheuer-Sturgeon
for German Language Services, Seattle, Washington
© 1998 by Harbor Press, Inc.
Illustrations © 1998 by Scott Bailey

Original German language edition titled
DIE FÜNF »TIBETER« – FEINSCHMECKER KÜCHE
© 1993 by Integral Verlag, an imprint of Scherz Verlag, Bern and Munich

Printed in the United States of America

10 9 8 7 6 5 4

Published by Harbor Press, Inc.
P.O. Box 1656
Gig Harbor, WA, 98335

ANCIENT SECRET

of the

FOUNTAIN OF YOUTH

COOKBOOK

*Simple, Delicious Recipes
for Health & Longevity*

About the Authors

❦

D R. DEVANANDO WEISE is well-known for his "non-diet" approach to harmonious, healthful nutrition. Together with his longtime companion Jenny P. Frederiksen, Weise has written this lively, practical nutrition and recipe book, loosely based on the dietary advice found in the popular *Ancient Secret of the Fountain of Youth, Book 1* (Doubleday, 1998) by Peter Kelder. Both authors live in Munich, Germany.

Dr. Weise was a lecturer and researcher for fifteen years at various German universities. Most recently, he taught at the University of Giessen. In his work, Dr. Weise draws on his extensive experience as a natural scientist, nutrition consultant, natural foods gourmet cook, geographer, and world traveler. He has published two other books in German, *Harmonische Ernährung (Harmonious Nutrition)*, 1990, and *Melone zum Fruhstück (Melon for Breakfast)*, 1991, and numerous articles. He frequently gives seminars and lectures on nutrition and self-awareness.

Jenny Frederiksen is also a natural foods gourmet cook, and she has a private practice in massage healing.

The authors are the creators of Gourmet's Garden, a popular natural foods restaurant in Munich, and Tabula Smaragdina Verlag, a publishing house, also in Munich.

CONTENTS

EATING FOR HIGH ENERGY AND HEALTHFUL LIVING

RECIPES

SALADS AND SALAD DRESSINGS

VEGETABLE DISHES AND SAUCES

Grain Dishes

Legumes

Vegetarian Patties and Burgers

Soups

Purées and Vegetarian Pâtés

Beverages

Desserts

Hors d'Oeuvres, Appetizers, and Snacks

Uncommon Ingredients

Index

A NOTE FROM THE PUBLISHER

ॐ

THIS COOKBOOK MAKES IT POSSIBLE for you to indulge in delicious, gourmet cuisine, without sacrificing simplicity and healthful nutrition. Its all-meatless recipes are a culinary treasure for anyone who revels in exciting flavors—vegetarians and meat-eaters alike.

While it stands on its own merits, this collection of recipes is the outgrowth of another book: *Ancient Secret of the Fountain of Youth* by Peter Kelder.

Kelder's book, which dates back to 1939, tells the story of a retired British Army Colonel, named Bradford, and his quest for the fabled fountain of youth. Colonel Bradford's search leads to the remote mountain wilderness of "forbidden Tibet" where he discovers an ancient monastery whose inhabitants have learned the secret of unending youth.

This secret, according to Bradford, is nothing more than a series of five simple, yoga-style exercises which he calls the Five Rites. He describes them in detail, and he also gives brief advice on other topics related to health and longevity.

One of these topics is diet and nutrition. Colonel Bradford argues for dietary simplicity, and he tells how to achieve optimal nutrition by combining the various kinds of foods you eat in a particular way.

While Kelder's book always enjoyed a loyal following, when it was updated and republished in the mid 1980s, it became phenomenally popular. Appearing in more than a dozen foreign language editions, and even in braille, *Ancient Secret of the Fountain of Youth* sold nearly two million copies around the world.

Nowhere was its popularity greater than in Germany, Austria, and Switzerland, where Kelder's book has remained on the best-seller lists for close to a decade.

Due to its popularity, the German language publisher, Integral Verlag, saw the need for a companion cookbook useful to readers of Colonel Bradford's dietary advice. As a result, Integral asked Devanando Otfried Weise and Jenny Frederiksen, well-known chefs and nutrition experts, to create the book which you now hold in your hands. In it, the authors blend useful information on diet and food combining with exciting, flavorful, vegetarian recipes gathered during their travels around the world.

This book is intended to help you launch your own culinary travels, right in your own kitchen. It will show you how simple, wholesome, healthful cooking can dazzle and thrill your senses, as it guides you on many memorable eating adventures.

Harry R. Lynn, Publisher

INTRODUCTION

❧

PERHAPS YOU HAVE ASKED yourself why the Five Tibetan Rites, the simple yoga-like exercises described in *Ancient Secret of the Fountain of Youth, Book 1* by Peter Kelder (Doubleday, 1998), are so popular. The answer is simple: they are uncomplicated and easy to perform, yet powerful enough to help you look and feel years younger, and gain a greater sense of well-being.

Most people who do these exercises regularly realize quickly that they are much more effective when accompanied by a diet based on the nutritional guidelines offered in the book. The guidelines are:

1. Never eat starch and meat at the same meal. (That is, follow the rules for keeping different types of food separate).

2. If coffee bothers you, drink it black, using no milk or cream. If it still bothers you, eliminate it from your diet.

3. Chew your food to a liquid, and cut down on the amount of food you eat.

4. Reduce the variety of foods you eat in one meal to a minimum.

As you might expect, however, we do not recommend that you take up the eating habits of Tibetan monks. This diet would be unsuitable for you because you live in a completely different environment and culture. And such a diet would be unnecessarily monotonous and limiting. The recipes in our book, therefore, are in keeping with the spirit of *Ancient Secret of the Fountain of Youth*: natural, simple meals prepared at home using fresh basic ingredients eaten slowly in a proper environment.

Working on a meal for hours using the sophisticated methods of master chefs does not necessarily improve a meal. Real gourmet cooking comes from the quality of the ingredients and careful attention to the natural flavors of foods. And the most nourishing, delicious foods are simple to prepare. When meals are simple the body receives clear signals and digests efficiently.

Yes, you can enjoy life and good food, and still have a healthy, energetic, disease-resistant body and a clear and alert mind. The food you eat to achieve this must be nutritious as well as delicious and satisfying. It must also cleanse and strengthen your body, mind, and spirit. Because no one diet is right for everyone, you must create your own individualized diet for good health and maximum satisfaction. This book will encourage you to figure out what works best for you, and will provide hints on how to do it.

There are 144 easy-to-follow recipes in this book. They are truly satisfying and nutritious. This is the food we serve in our gourmet snack bar in Munich, Gourmet's Garden, where every day we tempt hundreds of enthusiastic customers away from junk food. They opt instead for freshness, great taste, and good health.

Our book also provides a wealth of practical advice and tips for putting together meals and preparing food imaginatively. We will help you discover the proper, harmonious combinations of food that promote good health by offering important basic rules for nutrition that you can adapt to your own needs and tastes. We have put these nutritional guidelines at the beginning of the book to give you the background you need for the recipes that follow.

You will notice that, in some cases, we did not give exact amounts for ingredients. We did this whenever an exact amount was not needed to give you the freedom to experiment based on your own preferences. Recipes should always be adjusted to one's own taste.

Some of the ingredients included in our recipes might be unfamiliar to you, and some might be difficult to find. For your convenience, we have provided a list of uncommon ingredients at the back of the book to familiarize you with some of the less well-known ingredients and offer suggestions on where to purchase them and, where appropriate, how to make them yourself.

You will also find a list of the better seed catalogs and a list of suppliers of fresh herbs in case you're interested in ordering hard-to-find seeds by mail and growing some of your own ingredients, or ordering hard-to-find herbs.

This book is the product of years of experience. We are both natural scientists, health and nutrition counselors and teachers, and cooking instructors. We are also chefs and owners of a restaurant, so the recipes are based on practice as well as theory. Using detailed examples, we will show you which foods supply you with the best nutrients, and how to find truly satisfying foods for all occasions—foods that will make you feel good all over. You will see how much stronger and healthier you feel when you are no longer wasting energy digesting heavy and poorly put-together meals.

EATING FOR HIGH ENERGY

and

HEALTHFUL LIVING

Basic Principles of a Healthful Diet

※

THE MOST IMPORTANT PRINCIPLE *of a healthful diet is to prepare food yourself with fresh ingredients immediately before eating a meal using simple, gentle cooking methods.*[1] Once you have retrained yourself, the time you spend cooking will not be excessive. As any gourmet cook will tell you, it's not sophisticated, time-consuming cooking methods that produce great tasting food, but the freshness and quality of the ingredients. Food must be ripe, untreated, and, if possible, organically grown. If you do your own cooking, you will know where your ingredients come from and what happens to the food before you eat it. Your food will be free of all the additives used to manufacture products cheaply, to extend shelf life, and to change the taste in such a way that, unaware of your true needs, you end up overeating.

We recommend as your main foods fruits, vegetable fruits (tomatoes, cucumbers, bell peppers, zucchini, and avocados), vegetables, salads, sprouts, herbs, nuts, seeds, and cold-pressed oils. Your secondary foods should consist of a limited amount of grains, legumes, spices, sweet cream, and butter.

We advise you to avoid commercially-produced milk (pasteurized, sterilized, homogenized) and all other dairy products treated in this way. If you don't want to give up milk, we recommend unpasteurized (raw) milk and other dairy products, but use these sparingly. Most people can live without

---

1. Gentle cooking is cooking for a short time at low temperatures. This only partly destroys nutrients, as opposed to cooking for a long time or at high temperatures, which will take almost all the nutrients out of your food. Consume hot meals immediately because nutrients in hot food decrease drastically as time passes.

milk, cheese, yogurt, and other dairy products without damaging their health. For many people, dairy products are difficult to digest, and they cause the body to fill with mucus. In addition, some studies have shown that the calcium found in dairy products does not necessarily prevent osteoporosis. A well-known Chinese nutrition study found that osteoporosis barely exists in countries like China where they consume almost no dairy products. Harvey Diamond, author of the bestselling book, *Fit for Life*, tells us that the Chinese do not even have a word for osteoporosis.

Avoid eggs, fish, meat, and other animal products. Eat as little of these as possible, and always try to find animal products that have not been mass-produced or treated with chemicals.[2] *Above all, avoid pork and lunch meats.* Many studies of vegetarianism demonstrate that, all other things being equal, vegetarians are healthier than meat-eaters. They are even healthier than people who eat only small amounts of fish or meat once or twice a week. The primary reasons for this are:

1. *Meat contains poisons.* Animal products contain more additives than any other kind of food. These substances include environmental poisons, poisons found in animal fodder used on conventional farms or in the manufacturing process, and medicines and additives used in the animal-fattening process.

2. *Meat is hard to digest.* The human digestive system is not designed to cope with large amounts of animal products. As a result, it responds with acidity and illness (vascular ailments, heart disease, gout, rheumatism, arthritis, osteoporosis, fungus infections, and allergies).

The notion that a vegetarian diet will not provide you with the nutrition you need is unfounded. A vegetarian diet abounds in absolutely everything you need to be healthy, including all the amino acids needed to build necessary proteins. The right vegetarian meals eaten throughout the day will satisfy all your nutritional requirements. You do not need nutritional tables, calorie counters, or complicated formulas to prepare

---

2. Raw egg yolks, should, according to the latest research, not be eaten—not even if you live in the country and your eggs come directly from the nests of free-range chickens fed only on natural foods. Leave eggs alone, and instead eat nuts soaked overnight. The eggs sold in our markets are increasingly infected with salmonella, which can be fatal to humans. In addition, eggs which are more than a few hours old are contaminated with a variety of bacteria.

your meals. For example, you will get calcium in easily utilized form from fruits and vegetables as well as seeds such as sesame. There is plenty of iron in all green vegetables, and protein in fruit.

Avoid all foods that have been treated in any way. This includes white flour, polished rice, sugar, starch, extracted and refined oils, so-called soy meat, etc.

Avoid all preserved products. This includes fruits, vegetables, meat, sausage, fish, fruit juices, fruit drinks and other bottled and canned soft drinks, pasteurized milk, powdered milk or milk that needs no refrigeration, powdered eggs, etc. that contain preservatives of any kind. Exceptions include dried fruit if it has been carefully treated and, with some reservations, untreated frozen vegetables. Freezing ranks second to drying as the least damaging method of preservation.

Avoid all artificial preparations such as sweeteners and other flavorings, synthetic vitamins, and so-called seasonings, which are often confused with natural spices and seasonings.

Avoid all partially or completely precooked food products and ready-to-eat meals including most frozen foods. Turn your back on the food industry, and use ingredients you can buy directly from gardeners, farmers, organic food co-ops, health food stores, or your greengrocer.

Get into the habit of buying foods in season. Out-of-season vegetables and fruits are harvested before they are ripe and ready to be eaten. Many vegetables taste bland and have fewer nutrients when raised in a greenhouse out of season. Just think of the imported salad greens and tomatoes you get out of season and compare them to the sun-drenched tomatoes harvested from your own garden in season. It's worth taking the time to learn something about fruits and vegetables. There are many excellent illustrated books available on the subject.

Buy your fruits and vegetables from a retailer with whom you've built a personal relationship. If you know your grocer, you'll get good shopping advice and no one will try to sell you old produce. Find someone who will special-order for you. Look for a greengrocer who is not only a good businessperson, but who also has a feeling for genuine quality. Quality will vary tremendously in supermarkets and there is no substitute for a dealer who chooses his or her own produce.

Keep a supply of dried herbs and spices, and dried fruit. Besides the foods you buy for immediate consumption (fresh fruit, salads, vegetables, and herbs), keep an assortment of dried herbs and spices. Pepper, salt, and parsley, the most commonly used seasonings, are not the most important or the most valuable seasonings for your foods. Later on in the book, we will introduce you to several interesting spices and suggest imaginative ways to use them. You will enjoy the flavors and the benefits to your health. Also, always have dried fruit available so that when you want something sweet, you will have a choice between wholesome dried dates, for example, and unwholesome sweet chocolate.

Eat a combination of raw and cooked foods. If you want to lose weight, purify your blood, detoxify, revitalize, and heal yourself, we recommend that you include a large amount of raw food in your diet. However, a diet made up exclusively of raw foods is not healthful because your body will eventually need more nutrients than the foods you can eat raw will provide. The best diet is one that combines carefully handled cooked food with raw food, and is adapted to your own individual needs. In practice, the ratio of raw food to cooked food should look like this: 60% of what you eat should be raw, 20% should be gently cooked, and 20% should be cooked in the usual way (bread, legumes, cooked cereal, etc.).

Steamed vegetables with raw salad make a good combination. We suggest that you stir the steamed vegetables into your raw salad at the last moment, when the vegetables have cooled enough to eat. This also works well with puréed spinach. Sprinkle sprouts on top of your salad, or add chopped herbs, Chinese cabbage, or tomato wedges to enhance your meal. You can also combine a large raw salad with potatoes boiled in the skin or with brown rice. It is best to eat the raw food first, then the cooked.

Since eating habits are acquired in childhood, it is very difficult for most people to trade the beloved cooked, roasted, and baked dishes of their cuisine for a diet high in raw foods. At first, new dishes are not always as satisfying as the old ones. So we suggest that you add raw foods to your diet very gradually, while slowly learning to manage your health.

Make a slow transition to a vegetarian diet. Sometimes there are problems when changing over to a purely vegetarian diet. Some people who come from generations of meat-eaters have lost the ability to absorb enough nutrients from purely vegetarian foods. These people should change their diet slowly to prevent deficiencies. It may be many years (in some cases, even decades) until a purely vegetarian diet is sufficient, and no longer feels like sacrifice. On the other hand, many people were forced to eat meat as children and have always disliked it. As a rule, these people can make the change quickly and completely. Fortunately, thanks to hormone and salmonella scandals and a drastic decline in the quality of meat, meat consumption has decreased considerably over the last few years. Fruit and vegetable consumption has steadily increased over the last forty years.

The golden rule: Eat only as much as you need. Basically, you should learn to stop eating before you feel full. Yogis say that one quarter of the stomach should remain empty. Stated another way, food is simultaneously a blessing and a curse. Without food there is no life; with too much food, the quality and length of life are reduced. The mastery is finding the golden balance.

Think of your new way of eating as an incentive to experiment, instead of deprivation. You'll soon notice that you feel better when you reduce the total amount of food you eat, when you minimize animal products in your diet, and when you eat more raw foods.

Everyone needs a personalized diet, adapted to their individual lifestyle and preferences. Adapt our suggestions to your needs. True, we offer only vegetarian recipes here. This should encourage you to reduce the quantity of animal products in your diet as much as is reasonable for you, and to experiment with vegetables and raw foods. Success will follow naturally.

Fruits, Sprouts, Herbs, and Spices: The Enliveners

❦

WE ABSORB LARGE AMOUNTS of poison every day from our polluted surroundings and mass-produced food. More than ever we must take care to detoxify our bodies by drinking good water and, most important, eating fresh, ripe, raw fruit. Fruit contains large amounts of pure water and numerous vitamins, minerals, trace elements, and enzymes to stimulate and purify the body. In addition, fruits are the most easily and quickly digested foods, allowing the body time and energy for detoxification. Most of the energy supplied by concentrated foods (meat, grain products) is used up in digestion, so that there is little energy left for detoxification.

It is best to eat fruit by itself on an empty stomach to take full advantage of its quick and easy digestibility. Eaten alone, fruit remains in your stomach for only 15 to 20 minutes (depending on how well you chew it), and it provides energy almost immediately. You can, however, combine fruit with a green salad, celery, and vegetable fruits (tomatoes, cucumbers, bell peppers, zucchini, and avocados) and benefit from the combined energy of these additional foods. When you eat fruit with most other foods, or as a dessert, it remains in your stomach as long as all the rest. This might be many hours, during which time the sugar in the fruit can ferment and become harmful. If fruit on an empty stomach does not agree with you, it could be a sign that you are not healthy. Consult a nutritionist or someone skilled in the healing arts to find out what is wrong.

Eat several pieces of fruit each and every day. You can also plan to observe periodic "fruit only" days to detoxify and energize yourself. However, a long-term diet consisting only of fruit—whether for convenience or because you have been misinformed about the benefits—is not good, particularly if you gorge yourself on sweet fruit. Extremes are always harmful, so try to keep your diet balanced.

Sprouts for Energy

Sprouts, like fruit, are an excellent source of energy. Eat them raw to get the most from the nutrients they contain: live protein, enzymes, vitamins, minerals, trace elements. Sprouts are good in every kind of salad. Sprinkle 1 to 3 tablespoons of sprouts per person on every salad you prepare. You will find numerous ways to prepare sprout purées in the recipe section of this book. We do not, however, recommend meals consisting only of sprouts as this often causes digestive problems.

You can buy sprouts in most markets, and they are easy to grow at home. Any number of books will tell you how. This is what you do: Soak the seeds of spelt, lentils, or mung beans overnight in lots of lukewarm water. In the morning pour off the water and rinse the beans several times with fresh water. Let the seeds sit without water and rinse two or three times a day. By the third day, the sprouts will be long enough to eat. Refrigerate them to retard growth when they reach ⅛ to ¼ of an inch. If they are allowed to grow too long, they lose protein and nutrients. Keep sprouts in a covered pot or mason jar covered with cheesecloth. (You do not need a commercial sprouter.) Quinoa, an Indian grain, sprouts especially quickly (24 hours).

The Healing Effects of Herbs and Spices

Herbs improve the flavor of food and, because they are high in most valuable nutrients, they have great healing properties. Wild herbs such as ribwort, dandelion, daisy, sorrel, cress, dead nettle, stinging nettle, and coltsfoot have such high concentrations of nutrients that they make people fit, lively, and resistant to disease. If you have a balcony or a garden, you can easily grow a wide variety of herbs. Use herbs generously in salads and vegetable dishes.

Herbs and spices help to make digestion as easy and thorough as possible. Many stimulate digestive "fires," helping to burn toxins found in food. Some herbs warm the stomach and blood, increase appetite, and stimulate the senses. They often have an antibacterial or antiparasitic effect and strengthen the body's immune system. Many herbal remedies fight flatulence and stimulate peristaltic action (intestinal movement). Some help remove mucus and waste products from the stomach, intestines, lungs, and respiratory tract. In general, they stimulate digestion and circulation, and contribute to blood purification.

Here are descriptions of nine important herbs and spices, their possible healing effects on the body, and how to best use them in your diet.

Ginger

Fresh ginger root, available at most markets, is often called the "universal medicine." It is an excellent remedy for many ailments including colds and travel sickness, and it stimulates digestion. Slice it into thin strips and use it in hot dishes, grate it and sprinkle it on cooked dishes, or add it to salad dressings. Make a sandwich using slices of ginger, bread, and butter. Thinly sliced or grated, it can be added to hot water to make a stimulating, warming purification drink and is recommended for everyone who needs a warm drink on a winter morning. If you suffer from travel sickness, add a teaspoon of grated or thinly sliced ginger to a glass of warm water and drink it, including the ginger. Ginger can be very hot in soups, even without other sharp spices, so be careful not to use too much.

Turmeric

Turmeric and ginger are related. Turmeric is a mild digestive, and it simultaneously improves the intestinal flora and strengthens the liver. Turmeric remedies hyperfunction and hypofunction, and encourages the digestion of protein. It is found in all types of curry powder and is the source of its yellow color. You usually find turmeric as a yellow powder, but specialty shops, particularly Thai and other Southeast Asian grocery stores, sometimes sell fresh roots. These are good in sauces and soups.

Galagan

Galagan, also known as Thai or Laos ginger, is also a member of the ginger family. St. Elizabeth sings its praises in her writings. It has white roots with pink tips, and it has a strong medicinal taste. Along with ginger, lemon grass, and lemon leaves, it gives Thai sauces and soups their distinctive flavor. Galagan stimulates and warms the body, and causes perspiration. It is good for rheumatism, arthritis, aching joints, and helps to harmonize digestion. Fresh galagan is available in most Thai and other Southeast Asian grocery stores.

Cardamom

Cardamom is another member of the ginger family. We use the seeds of the cardamom plant rather than the roots. Cardamom is one of the best and most easily tolerated aids to digestion, especially when used with fennel. It stimulates the spleen and "fans the digestive fires." When added to milk, it reduces the formation of mucus. Add ½ of a crushed cardamom seed to coffee to neutralize caffeine toxins. This also adds an interesting flavor to the coffee. The mixture of cardamom, fennel, and cinnamon is characteristic of cooking in Kashmir.

Asant

Asant, also called Asafetida, or "stinking asant," is the resin or secretion of a tropical plant. It is a powerful stimulant, and it prevents flatulence, clears the intestines of old excrement, gets rid of parasites, stabilizes intestinal flora, and eases cramps and pain. Asant works much like garlic, but it is more effective. It makes lentil and bean dishes easier to digest. Use asant with ginger and cardamom, or cumin and coriander. Garlic, asant, ginger powder, and chili fight stomach and intestinal candida infections.

Cilantro

Cilantro (fresh coriander leaves) works to cool the body. It resembles parsley and is easy to grow. Cilantro is very popular and is frequently used in Indian and Southeast Asian kitchens, giving the traditional smooth flavor to their dishes. Cilantro is often used with cumin and fennel to help alleviate intestinal problems. When combined, these three spices make a good seasoning for white cabbage.

Garlic

Volumes have been written about the healing effects of garlic. People have used it successfully for thousands of years to treat numerous ailments. Garlic is especially recommended for meat-eaters, since it improves digestion and lowers blood pressure, cholesterol levels, and triglycerides. Some people report that it prevents blood clots and the cardiac and circulatory problems that threaten meat-eaters. In addition, garlic stimulates the immune system and fights bronchitis and other infections, and colds.

Cayenne

Cayenne stimulates circulation and intestinal "fires," and it is also believed to have a cleansing and strengthening effect on the lungs, promoting ejection of sputum, alleviating chronic bronchitis, and helping to dissolve blood clots.

Mixed Spices

Indian curry powder is the most well-known mix of spices. There are endless varieties of curry powder; try this recipe for starters:

> 8 oz. coriander seed
> 1 ½ tsp. each cumin, black mustard seed,
>   fenugreek seed, and black peppercorn
> 20 dried curry leaves
> 15 dried chili peppers
> 3 tbs. turmeric powder

Roast the first 5 spices briefly in a pan to bring out the flavor and render the curry less perishable. Set aside to cool. Then grind or crush the mixture with curry leaves and chili peppers in a spice grinder, coffee grinder, or mortar. If you prefer a mild curry powder, leave out the chili peppers. Add the turmeric powder last. Your dishes will be most successful if you prepare a fresh mix of spices for each meal.

Garam Masala is the Indian name for mixed spices that warm the body. Most of the spices used in the above recipe are used in Garam Masala in varying quantities. Garam Masala with turmeric is used mostly in southern India, and Garam Masala without turmeric is more common in northern India.

Proper Food Combining, Preparation, and Menu Planning

❧

Though the human body somehow manages to digest the most amazing combinations of food, human digestion works most effectively, effortlessly, and completely when different kinds of food are not mixed. As Colonel Bradford writes in *Ancient Secret of the Fountain of Youth, Book 1* (Doubleday,1998), "Reduce the variety of foods you eat in one meal to a minimum." It is actually more accurate to refer to food groups, rather than foods, because it is easy, for example, to digest a mixed salad.

Proper Combinations

Certain combinations of food are particularly easy to digest, relieve stress, and help to purify and energize the body. (For a detailed discussion of proper food combining see *Ancient Secret of the Fountain of Youth, Book 2*, Doubleday, 1998.) Some of these combinations are:

- Cheese with salad and vegetables
- Fish with vegetables
- Steak and salad
- Omelet with vegetables and salad

These combinations will not make you feel exhausted and heavy after a meal, but will give you renewed energy. We easily absorb the nutrients provided by these combinations, and we require minimal energy for digestion, leaving more energy available for purification, detoxification, and weight loss. There is no fermentation or putrefaction during the digestive process, and no damaging substances are produced.

The concept of "balanced meals" is well known and usually refers to meals that contain all vital nutrients. No one bothers to ask, however, if these nutrients are easy for the body to digest and use. Because the typical "balanced meal" includes foods from several different food groups, the meal cannot be properly digested, so the nutrients in the food cannot be properly absorbed and used by the body. Therefore, it is not necessary or desirable for all required nutrients to be present in every meal. You will get the proper amount of every necessary nutrient by eating a variety of meals with an emphasis on different foods at each meal. This is much more efficient than eating "balanced mixtures" that are hard to digest. For example, a meal of unpeeled potatoes and a salad may not contain every essential amino acid, but it is easy to digest and the nutrients can be readily used by the body. You can compensate for the lack of amino acids by having an omelet or legumes for dinner. The body will store the nutrients it needs from each meal.

The combination of foods that puts the greatest stress on the body is the traditional mixture of starch and concentrated protein such as:

- Meat or fish and noodles, potatoes, rice or dumplings
- Bread and cheese (a combination acceptable
  only if the cheese is more than 60% fat)
- Pizza dough with salami and/or cheese
  (heated cheese is often very difficult to digest)

Correct Food Combining

Choose food combinations with only two closely-related food groups at each meal.

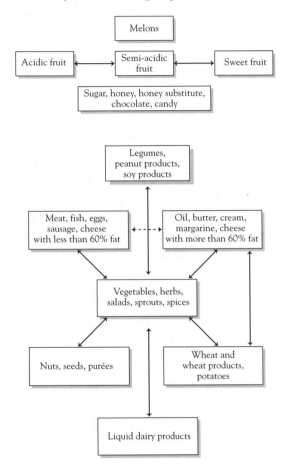

This is the right way to combine foods! Choose a combination of two groups of foods from those that are directly connected. Avoid combining acidic foods (for example, tomato sauce) with carbohydrates (for example, noodles) because this combination impedes the digestion of carbohydrates (starch).

Properly Combined Full-Course Meals

When planning a menu, first decide whether you want a meal based primarily on protein or carbohydrates. If your guests are not complete vegetarians, go for protein.

Protein-Based Menu

Appetizer: Pineapple, papaya, mango cocktail (These fruits are rich in special enzymes that help protein digestion.)

Fifteen-minute break

Soup: Raw tomato soup
Main Course: Ginger coconut sauce
with vegetables and tempeh chips
Dessert: Avocado cream

Carbohydrate-Based Menu

Appetizer: Fruit salad of pears, peaches, and blueberries

Fifteen-minute break

Soup: Cream of raw carrot
Main Course: Green beans and rice
Dessert: Cream of millet with honey and fresh ginger

Carbohydrates, especially complex carbohydrates such as grain products, give you energy and endurance. Unlike sugar, they release energy slowly.

The Daily Rhythm of Meals

When and what you eat at different times of the day is important. The human body runs on a daily cycle, and it is worth paying attention to this cycle if sound digestion is important to you.

Breakfast

We recommend that you start the day with a glass of water. Any mild, soft water will do as long as it is as low in minerals as possible. Steam-distilled water purifies and detoxifies the best. It is a good idea to pour the water into glass bottles and let it stand several hours in the sun before drinking. We recommend that you "charge" the water with sunlight and drink it promptly, as we do with all bottled and tap water. Drink water at room temperature, warm, or hot depending on your mood and the time of year. You can drink water plain, with freshly grated ginger, or with a few splashes of lemon juice. If you prefer herbal tea, that is all right, too. Just change the flavor frequently. Vegetable broth and miso soup are especially welcome in winter.

After your morning exercise (perhaps the Five Tibetan Rites), you may drink fruit juice or eat fruit according to your taste and the season. Fruit purifies and detoxifies, and it is so easy to digest that it does not rob the body of necessary energy. If you eat a traditional breakfast, your body requires so much energy to digest it that no further purification is possible. Not only that, but you'll need coffee to wake you up.

In the course of several weeks or months, you will learn to delay having anything other than fruit and water in the morning until you can last until noon. You will benefit greatly from drinking water and eating fruit in the morning, but it is up to you to determine how much fruit is good for you. If, in spite of thorough chewing and eating on an empty stomach, you find you cannot tolerate fruit, seek medical advice.

Lunch

Since midday is the time of day when you have the greatest digestive strength, lunch should be your main meal. It is the time for salad, vegetables, and raw roots. Completely healthy people, blessed with a robust digestive system, can eat raw roots in the evening without difficulty as long as they chew thoroughly. However, most people who eat raw food in the evening have digestive problems because it stays in the stomach too long and may begin to ferment. The digestive process is too slow in the evening for most people, and it functions inefficiently.

Eating raw food for lunch is a good idea for people who work during the day where there are no cooking facilities. Take washed whole cucumbers, tomatoes, green peppers, avocados, celery, and carrots, and have them for lunch or nibble them during your break instead of eating harmful cafeteria food. Prepare a dip or dressing in the morning or the night before for your lunchtime vegetables (see recipe section). You can also prepare a mixed salad with sprouts. If raw food isn't enough for you, bring some bread and butter or soaked nuts to go with it.

At around four o'clock in the afternoon, you might have tea and dried fruit as a snack.

Dinner

In the evening, prepare a warm meal with steamed or stir-fried vegetables and a small bowl of soaked grain, preferably non-acidic millet or buckwheat. Of course, you can vary the kinds of grain you eat. Variety is always beneficial! It makes sense to eat grain in the evening because then it is most likely to promote the feeling of total satiety so pleasing to our nerves and emotions. Otherwise, you might suddenly feel voracious at around eight o'clock or later, raid the refrigerator or pantry, and ruin all your good work. For most people the hardest time to stick to a healthful diet is in the evening. A well-rounded, complete evening meal will prevent disaster. Of course, you can eat something from the dessert section of this book at the end of your evening meal. Some of the desserts are suitable for lunch at work as well.

The Most Beneficial Cooking Methods

The best cooking methods, called "gentle cooking," are: Chinese stir-fry, poaching in juice with a little fat, steaming, and simmering grains after bringing them briefly to a boil. These low-temperature, relatively quick cooking methods ensure that the foods you're cooking retain their nutrients and do not absorb a wide range of harmful substances, from hot fat to radiation from microwave ovens. There are pots on the market equipped with thermostats and designed to cook gently at the low temperature of 212° F. You'll find many examples of foods cooked using these gentle cooking methods in the recipe section of this book.

Keep in mind that it is unnecessary to cook vegetables and noodles until they are soft. Once you have changed your old habits, you will find that they taste much better and are much healthier when they are tender and crunchy, or al dente. Foods lose most of their nutrients when they are cooked too long and at temperatures that are too high.

Avoid the following cooking methods, which at the very least destroy nutrients, and at worst are damaging to your health and can be carcinogenic: deep frying, prolonged roasting in hot fat, broiling, prolonged baking at high temperatures (in bread, for example, damaging substances remain in the crust), cooking until food is mushy. Avoid eating food cooked in microwave ovens; they completely destroy nutrients and they use food as a "transmitter," potentially doing long-term damage to your health.

Helpful Kitchen Equipment

Pots and Pans

The best pots to use are gold, then glass (heat-proof Pyrex, for example), then enamel, then steel. Aluminum is totally unacceptable; it is harmful to your health and should not be used under any circumstances.

The Vegetable Knife

Japanese vegetable knives are unsurpassable for cutting vegetables. They are available in health food stores and kitchen specialty shops. Japanese knives are large, with very sharp rectangular blades. Chrome, vanadium, and stainless steel blades are the best.

Professional cooks hold the knife against the knuckles. The slicing motion should be smooth and natural. Keep knives very sharp in order to avoid too much back and forth sawing and squeezing. For sharpening, buy a flat whet stone in a size appropriate for the knife. Ask a salesperson to show you how to use it. Keep knives separate from other kitchen utensils in the original boxes, cartons, or wooden knife holders to make sure the blades don't become jagged and no one gets cut rummaging through drawers.

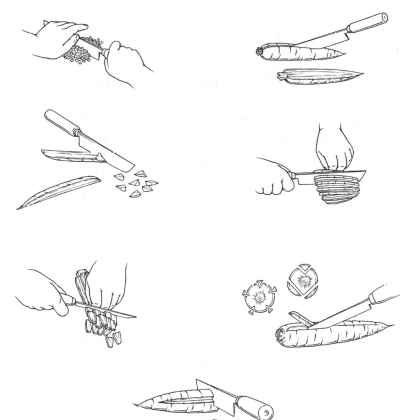

With some practice, you will double your cutting speed and confidence, and be proud of the results. You can cut vegetables any way you

like, into any size and shape. Just make sure you are consistent so everything takes the same amount of time to cook. Start firm vegetables before softer ones so they all cook evenly.

The Chinese Wok

Vegetarian cooks quickly discover the pleasure of a Chinese wok, which makes it easy to cook vegetables simply and quickly. When shopping for a wok, make sure to get one that fits your range. A wok designed for gas will not fit an electric range. Buy a cover and a wooden spatula at the same time.

The Mortar

It is a good idea to buy a large, sturdy mortar. Thai stores sell heavy stone mortars with big, stout pestles made of the same material. Mortars this big and heavy are perfect for crushing vegetables. Curry paste with fresh ingredients, Italian pesto, and small quantities of ground nuts are easy to prepare in a heavy mortar. Little china mortars are usually not very useful since you have to hold them with one hand, and the little pestle is only good for grinding large seeds like coriander. A coffee mill works very well for large quantities of dried spices. It is a good idea to buy spices whole and grind them just before you need them to preserve the delicate aroma longer.

The Vegetable Grater

We recommend a grater for preparing raw food. To grate large quantities, use a manual mill. Graters are available with a variety of blades and they have been around for decades. Use an electric food processor with accessories for chopping vegetables only when cooking for a large crowd.

The Vegetable Brush

Scrub fruits and vegetables with a brush very thoroughly before eating. Organic vegetable shops sell Japanese vegetable brushes, which are particularly good for cleaning root vegetables and potatoes.

The Juice Extractor

For extracting juice or puréeing, we recommend a Champion juicer or any other juicer available that actually presses the juice, rather than extracting by centrifugal action. The centrifugal juicers on the market fail to fulfill their purpose; they do not deliver healthful juices full of nutrients. Experiments conducted by German oncologist Dr. Max Gerson, prove that centrifugal action destroys curative power by deforming vital molecules, rendering them ineffective. Champion juice extractors purée fruit, vegetables, nuts, and seeds gently.

RECIPES

All the recipes in this book

serve 3-4 people.

Use the following equivalents for herbs and spices:
1 tbs. fresh herbs or spices equals
1 tsp. dried herbs or spices equals
¾ tsp. ground powdered herbs or spices

SALADS

and

SALAD DRESSINGS

*The following dressings complete your salads
or raw vegetables in the most delicious way.
Try all kinds of dressings and you won't be bored.*

LEMON VINAIGRETTE

❧

½ cup sunflower oil or your choice of cold-pressed oil

Juice of ¼ to ½ lemon (depending upon size)
or lime (especially delicious)

Pepper and herb salt, to taste

Chopped herbs, to taste

We will start with this classic, simple dressing, which you can vary by adding herbs in season. Use herbs generously. As you know, they do more than add wonderful flavor. Before adding herbs, use a small whisk to beat the dressing until it emulsifies.

Lovage is particularly good with this recipe. Or try freshly grated ginger.

ITALIAN DRESSING

½ cup cold-pressed olive oil

2 tbs. balsamic vinegar

Pepper, to taste

Herb salt, to taste

1 clove garlic

1 tsp. mustard

Olives, finely chopped, to taste (optional)

Fresh basil, to taste (optional)

Capers, chopped, to taste (optional)

Combine first four ingredients, and beat well. It's worth spending the extra money for real Italian balsamic vinegar, or organic apple cider vinegar. Then pierce garlic clove several times with a fork. Ten minutes before dinner, add it to the dressing for aroma. Then remove garlic so its flavor will not be too strong.

This dressing can be enhanced by adding finely chopped olives and fresh basil. Add 1 teaspoon mustard to thicken the dressing and stabilize the emulsion. Add chopped capers for a zesty alternative.

In Europe and the United States, mass-produced food contains a great deal of vinegar. This is bad for the kidneys. Limit the amount of vinegar you use. Citric acid from citrus fruit is a much healthier substitute. You can also use sauerkraut juice in salads as a vinegar substitute.

GREEN GODDESS DRESSING

❦

½ cup organic yogurt   *½ cup sour cream*

Paprika, to taste   *Pepper, to taste*

Herb salt, to taste   *Chopped herbs, to taste*

Blend all ingredients well, adding plenty of minced dill, parsley and chives. Also add small amounts of borage, lovage, marjoram, and thyme, but if any of these herbs are not available, simply use your own combinations. The first three herbs are the most important.

It's best to make this dressing in a food processor with a chopping attachment. For thicker consistency, add mayonnaise. Green Goddess Dressing also goes extremely well with warm, steamed, or poached vegetables.

❦

If you don't want to use dairy products use the non-dairy version of this recipe for a strictly vegetarian Green Goddess.

1 cup nuts and seeds
(almonds, cashews, shelled sunflower seeds,
sesame seeds) or preserved almond or nut purée.

½ – 1 cup water depending on desired consistency
(do not use the soaking water)

Herbs and spices listed above

If you're using nuts and seeds, soak them overnight. Purée the first two ingredients in the blender, add herbs and spices, and purée again.

With or without dairy products, this dressing is light and tastes divine (hence the name).

31

GOURMET'S GARDEN DRESSING

❦

We invented this dressing for our vegetarian snack bar and catering service, Gourmet's Garden, in Munich. In this recipe, olive oil from southern Europe and Japanese plum wine join in a surprisingly harmonious blend. Japanese plum wine is the juice of umeboshi plums (actually apricots) and shisho leaves, fermented in lactic acid. It contains salt, so there is no need to add any more to the dressing. It is very good on steamed vegetables, and is frequently used in macrobiotic diets.

❦

½ cup cold-pressed olive oil

2–3 tbs. Japanese plum wine

¼ cup cream (optional)

Pepper, to taste (optional)

Blend the first two ingredients thoroughly. Place the Japanese plum wine in a food processor or blender and very slowly, almost drop by drop, add the olive oil. If you like, add a little pepper.

If you want a creamy consistency, like thin mayonnaise, keep stirring while you add ¼ cup cream in a thin stream. If the taste of Japanese plum wine is too weak, add more.

This thick, creamy dressing is fantastic. We mix it with diced celery, zucchini, tomatoes, and avocado. Sometimes the dressing remains watery no matter how much it is stirred. No one knows why. It simply doesn't emulsify. Don't give up. It will work the next time.

SEED AND NUT DRESSINGS

❧

These dressings are made with freshly puréed seeds (sesame,
for example) or nuts (hazelnuts, almonds, cashews) diluted with liquid
and seasoned however you like. A popular nut and seed blend
consists of 1 part almonds, 2 parts shelled sunflower seeds,
and 1 part sesame seeds (optional).

❧

Cover the seeds or nuts with water and soak overnight. The next day
discard the soaking water and rinse the seeds or nuts well.

If you like, you can soak a variety of seeds and nuts together. Walnuts,
however, should be soaked by themselves since they will discolor other
nuts. Almonds, hazelnuts, walnuts, and pumpkin seeds must be soaked
for at least 12 hours; cashews and sesame seeds need only 4 to 6 hours;
sunflower seeds need 8. If you wish, you can remove the skins from
almonds after soaking them. After soaking, purée the seeds and nuts in a
blender adding water or vegetable juice in a thin stream until the sauce
reaches the consistency you desire.

If you are making only a small amount of dressing, use a mortar and
pestle instead of a blender. Finally, blend in spices or herbs. Experiment
with different kinds. Try ground cardamom, for example, or fennel,
or even cloves and cinnamon.

Puréed sesame seed dressings are traditionally seasoned with lemon
juice, garlic, parsley, pepper and salt. In some parts of the Middle East,
ground cumin makes for an interesting variation in taste. Tahini, or
sesame seed purée, is especially popular in Arab countries and in Israel
where it is diluted with milk instead of water. This creates a thick,
creamy sauce which is eaten with unleavened bread (pita), vegetables,
or salad.

Gourmet Dressing

❧

The following recipe is a specialty of ours and contains no acidic
ingredients. This is important because an enzyme found in saliva
called ptyalin inhibits the digestion of starch if there is acid present.
Therefore, this dressing goes extremely well with brown rice,
(which can be combined with gomasio: 9 parts ground,
roasted sesame seeds and 1 part sea salt) and vegetables
that contain starch, such as carrots (5% starch).
It is also excellent with steamed vegetables.

❧

½ cup sesame oil

2 tbs. sesame oil made from roasted sesame seeds
(see Uncommon Ingredients, page 199)

¼ cup cream

2-3 tbs. tamari or soy sauce

Ginger root (optional)

Blend the ingredients well in a blender or food processor,
adding the oils last.

Blend the oils with the other ingredients very slowly, almost drop by
drop. For more flavor, add grated or fresh ginger root cut into thin strips.

Sesame is high in easily utilized calcium. If you are worried about
osteoporosis, sesame is important for you. Remember, though, that
sesame seed that has not been ground cannot be properly digested.
Gomasio and tahini are good sources of sesame.

VITALITY DRESSING

Celery, several ribs

1 avocado

Lemon juice, to taste

Pepper, to taste

Herb salt, to taste

Chopped herbs, to taste

Using a juicer, extract the juice from several ribs of celery, and purée it with one avocado. Season with lemon juice, pepper, and herb salt. Add chopped herbs to taste. The consistency can vary from thick to thin.

If you wish, purée the avocado with water instead of celery juice. You can also purée the avocado with carrot juice and season with cumin, pepper, and herb salt.

This dressing is made from raw ingredients and is therefore high in valuable vitamins, enzymes, and minerals.

INDIAN SALAD DRESSING

❧

Devanando first tasted this dressing during his trips to northern India,
along the borders of the Himalayas near Palampur and Dharmsala.
The taste of cumin and ginger gives it its distinctive flavor.
(Cumin is a variety of caraway, but don't confuse the two.
They are related but taste very different.)

❧

½ cup sesame oil

¼ cup cream

2 tbs. lime (preferred) or lemon juice

½ garlic clove, crushed (or according to taste)

1 tsp. freshly grated ginger root

½ tsp. ground cumin

1 tsp. honey

Pepper, to taste

Salt, to taste

Stir all ingredients thoroughly. Garnish salad with fresh coriander leaves
(cilantro).

Chinese Dressing

❦

This dressing is best as a marinade for steamed vegetables.
It is excellent with eggplant (see pages 61–62), soy sprouts,
white cabbage, and Chinese cabbage.

❦

¼ cup dry sherry or rice wine

3 tbs. soy sauce

¼ cup lemon juice

3 tbs. sesame oil

3 tbs. oil of roasted sesame

1 clove garlic, crushed

¼ cup fresh ginger root, cut into thin strips

1 tsp. honey

Salt, to taste

Sesame seeds to garnish the salad

Blend all ingredients.

Thai Dressing

❦

The following dressing is prepared warm, but it can also be served
chilled, especially for salads made with cooked vegetables

❦

1 cup water

*⅓ cup coconut cream (more or
less, according to desired consistency)*

1 tsp. vegetable granules

*¼ tsp. ground cardamom seeds
(open the pods and remove the
seeds)*

*½ tsp. grated or minced
Thai ginger*

*Fresh turmeric
or ½ tsp. turmeric powder*

*4 lemon leaves
cut in very thin strips*

*1 fresh chili pepper,
without seeds, or a small
amount chili powder
(optional)*

*Herb salt, pepper,
and lemon juice for seasoning
(optional)*

Heat the water and blend in the coconut cream and vegetable granules.
Add the rest of the ingredients, and let the dressing cool, or use it at
once with cooked vegetables.

This recipe calls for thickened coconut cream, which is available in
Thai markets and even in some supermarkets. Coconut milk has a wonderful flavor and a creamy consistency, which makes it a good substitute
for cream. It is an excellent alternative for people who do not use milk
and dairy products in cooking!

This recipe also calls for lemon leaves. The Thai are fond of lemon leaves,
the peel of a special type of lemon, and lemon grass for seasoning. These
impart a lemony flavor without acidity. Lemon grass is best suited for
soups. For dressings and sauces we particularly recommend lemon leaves,
available fresh in Thai markets, which keep in the freezer for a long time.
They go well with grated lemon peel (from unsprayed lemons, of course).

Free-style Pesto

Substitute your own creative ideas for this famous Italian pesto recipe made with olive oil, garlic, Parmesan, pine nuts, basil, salt, and pepper. The basic recipe remains the same, but you can create variations on the theme using available ingredients.

The basic sauce consists of 1 cup cold-pressed olive oil, and 1–2 bunches of garden herbs to taste including basil, parsley, dill, thyme, tarragon, sage, lovage, and coriander. Go easy on the coriander and lovage. Some people find them too overpowering. Mixed herbs work well.

Mince the herbs very well and blend them with oil in a mortar. Season with pepper and herb salt to taste. The mixture should have a purée-like consistency. You can add water to thin out, if you wish.

Serve with salad, cooked vegetables, or noodles. This is good as a dip for baguettes and is excellent with Italian salad.

Pesto can be enriched with nuts, almonds, sunflower seeds or pine nuts, ground or pounded in a mortar. You can also use preserved nut purée.

Add crushed garlic in this variation if you love garlic, but beware: garlic reaches its full potential in this mixture.

For variety, add a little grated cheese. Or use cheese in place of spices. You can control the consistency of the sauce by the amount of olive oil or water you add.

Add a teaspoon of prepared mustard, half a crushed garlic clove, and three tablespoons of lemon juice to the basic sauce for a third variation.

Fresh Chutney (Sambal)

❦

Finally, here is a recipe for fresh chutney (also known as sambal),
a dressing that stimulates both appetite and digestion.
It is often served in Ceylon and southern India.

❦

1 cup unsweetened shredded coconut

*1–2 minced chili peppers, with or without seeds
depending on how hot you want it*

¼ cup grated fresh ginger root

Juice of 1 lime (preferred) or lemon

1 small red onion, minced

¼ tsp. herb salt

Pound all the ingredients in a large mortar.

Vary the flavor by adding a bunch of minced cilantro (fresh coriander leaves), fresh mint, parsley, or garlic, to taste.

This chutney is especially good served with vegetable or grain dishes. If you go to dinner in Sri Lanka (Ceylon) and order one of the local curries, you will probably get a fresh chutney like this one. Preserved chutney (usually made in England) is available in many forms.

And now to the salad recipes…

MIXED GREEN SALAD

❧

Every mixed salad should include leaf lettuces (head lettuce, iceberg lettuce, endive, romaine and oak leaf, lollo rosso, radicchio, chicory, lamb's lettuce, arugula, and dandelion). All alone, with the simple addition of some sprouts and herbs and maybe a few radish slices for color, leaf lettuces make a splendid salad. (See Dressings, pages 29–40.) Be especially lavish when adding garden herbs or wild herbs to your salad.

Leaf lettuce does not necessarily have to be chopped, but always make sure it is absolutely fresh.

RATATOUILLE

❧

This salad combines easily-digested raw vegetable fruits, such as bell peppers (any color), cucumbers, tomatoes, zucchini, and avocado. If sweet red onions agree with you, use them to decorate your salad. Toss with Italian Dressing (see page 30), Gourmet's Garden Dressing (see page 32), or Vitality Dressing (see page 35).

Add chopped herbs of your choice.

JAPANESE PLUM WINE SALAD
from
GOURMET'S GARDEN

꽃

1 medium zucchini, diced

2 ribs celery, sliced

3 tomatoes, coarsely diced

1 avocado, diced

Mix all ingredients and marinate them in Gourmet's Garden Dressing (see page 32).

CHINESE CABBAGE SALAD WITH CASHEW NUTS

꽃

1 medium Chinese cabbage, thinly sliced

4 tomatoes, diced

¼ cup mung bean sprouts

¼ cup cashew nuts, coarsely chopped

Mix ingredients and marinate in Gourmet Dressing (see page 34).

WATERCRESS SALAD

½ lb. or 5 cups watercress (stems discarded)

3 ribs celery, sliced

1 bunch radishes, sliced

¼ cup walnuts

Mix ingredients and marinate in Italian Dressing (see page 30).

Use raspberry vinegar in the dressing instead of balsamic vinegar. This makes a particularly delicious, extravagant salad, which you absolutely have to try. To delight your friends' palates even more, dot the salad with small bits of brie cheese.

Marinated Mushrooms

1 lb. or 6 cups mushrooms

½ cup cold-pressed olive oil

¼ cup lemon juice, freshly squeezed

½ clove garlic, pressed

1 bunch parsley

1 tsp. Dijon mustard

½ tsp. herbs de Provence

Herb salt, to taste

Pepper, freshly ground, to taste

Cut the mushrooms in four or eight pieces, depending on size. Marinate in the dressing made of the remaining ingredients. If you wish, marinate other vegetables as well. This is an excellent dish for a cold buffet, or as an omelet filling.

SHIITAKE AND LAMB'S LETTUCE SALAD

❧

Shiitake mushrooms are very flavorful Japanese tree mushrooms
that grow on oaks and birches. They are available dried in
Asian markets and fresh in most vegetable markets.
For this recipe, we use fresh mushrooms.

❧

½ lb. or 3 cups lamb's lettuce

*¼ lb. or 2 ½ cups fresh Shiitake mushrooms,
cut into bite-size pieces*

1 cup wheat sprouts or spelt sprouts

½ cup roasted pine nuts

Thin, raw carrot sticks

Spread a layer of lamb's lettuce on a serving plate. Cover with Shiitake
mushrooms, sprouts, and pine nuts. Moisten the salad with Chinese
Dressing (see page 37). Garnish with thin carrot sticks.

In 1969, an American physician, Dr. Kenneth Cochran of the University of Michigan, discovered that Shiitake mushrooms contain valuable
substances that fight viral infections and strengthen the immune system.
Some report that Shiitake mushrooms lower blood cholesterol levels and
reduce the harmful effects of saturated fats.

SUMMER SALAD

🐦

This unusual combination from our catering service is easy
to digest. It's also an exotic taste experience. Try it!

🐦

2 bananas, sliced

1 large or 2 small mangos, pit removed, diced

3 tomatoes, halved and cut into 8 pieces

2 avocados, pit removed, diced

Marinate all ingredients in Vitality Dressing (see page 35). This salad
tastes good even without dressing.

FRUIT SALAD
with
BANANA PEACH DRESSING AND MINT

Choose your favorite fruits. Dice and mix for fruit salad.

Purée banana and a ripe, juicy peach in a blender (add a little water for desired consistency). Pour this banana dressing over the fruit salad.

Decorate with peppermint leaves. Eat the salad at once before the dressing discolors.

You can make fruit dressing from any number of fruits. Just purée them with a little freshly squeezed juice or water. Children especially enjoy fruit salad prepared this way.

Remember not to mix sweet and sour fruits. You may add dried fruit if you like.

Leaf Lettuce
with
Citrus Fruits and Nuts

%

This salad can be made with a variety of different ingredients. One popular version is a mix of chicory, oranges or tangerines, and chopped walnuts or hazelnuts. Whipped cream makes a good dressing.

Grapefruit, lamb's lettuce, and almonds make another good combination. Soak the almonds, or any other nuts, in warm water overnight. This makes them more digestible and enhances the flavor. Soaking makes the nuts crunchy, and they taste as if they have just been picked off a tree or bush.

Raw Carrot and Apple Salad

%

½ lb. or 2 cups carrots, thinly grated

1 ripe apple, grated

½ cup raisins or currants

¼ cup shredded coconut

¼ cup ground sesame seeds

¼ cup sesame oil

Mix all ingredients.

Red Beet and Apple Salad

✺

A delicious salad from Denmark, one of our favorites!

✺

½ lb. or 2 cups red beets, grated

2 apples, grated

5 oz. sour cream

½ cup sunflower seeds

1 tbs. honey

Mix beets and apples with sour cream. Put a portion of the salad on each plate.

Roast sunflower seeds gently in a small, dry skillet. Remove skillet from heat and add honey, which will liquefy and coat the sunflower seeds. Pour this mixture over the salad.

This salad does not precisely follow the rules of proper food combining (see pages 14–17), but it is so delicious that we wanted you to try it. Just make sure you chew it well for good digestion, and everything will be fine.

Red beets are high in vitamin C and iron.

Fresh Spinach Salad
with
Avocados and Mushrooms

❦

*½ lb. or 8 cups fresh spinach,
torn or cut into bite-size pieces*

¼ lb. or 1 cup mushrooms, sliced

3 tomatoes, diced

1 avocado, diced

Toss and marinate all the ingredients in Italian Dressing (see page 30).

Jerusalem Artichoke and Almond Creation

½ lb. or 1½ cups Jerusalem artichokes, coarsely grated

1 cup almonds, soaked overnight and coarsely chopped

1 bunch radishes, sliced

¼ bunch parsley, minced

Steam Jerusalem artichokes very lightly or leave them raw.

Marinate either raw or steamed Jerusalem artichokes, almonds, and radishes in Gourmet Dressing (see page 34) or simply in oil and lemon juice. Garnish with parsley.

Jerusalem artichokes are related to sunflowers. If you boil them, the fructose and most of the flavor are lost in the cooking water, leaving you with rather dull-tasting tubers.

Romaine Lettuce Rolls
with
Sprouts and Puréed Avocado

❦

2 avocados

Fresh, mixed herbs, minced, to taste

Juice of ½ lemon

Pepper, to taste

Herb salt, to taste

*½ lb. or 4 ¾ cups fresh alfalfa sprouts
or 1 cup lentil sprouts*

1 head romaine lettuce, leaves separated

Mash the first five ingredients with a fork. Place a tablespoon of this purée and some sprouts on a lettuce leaf, and roll it lengthwise. Do this at the table so you can pop the finished rolls in your mouth at once.

If you want to make the rolls ahead of time, place them very closely together so they don't come undone. You can also pin them with a toothpick.

Romaine lettuce is very crunchy and contrasts wonderfully with the creamy taste of avocados.

Radish with Cottage Cheese and Paprika

8 oz. or 1 cup cottage cheese

1 large radish, coarsely grated

Paprika, to taste

Pepper, to taste

Herb salt, to taste (optional)

Fresh herbs for garnish

Mix cottage cheese with grated radish and season with paprika, pepper, and salt to taste. Garnish the salad with fresh herbs.

This unusual salad tastes good and is filling. It makes a nice snack.

CABBAGE ITALIAN STYLE

*1 lb. or 4 cups young, tender white cabbage,
sliced very thinly*

½ tsp. ground caraway

½ tsp. ground fennel

Marinate all ingredients in Italian Dressing (see page 30).

Pound marinated cabbage with a potato masher. Let stand, covered, for several hours. Naturally, you can eat it immediately if you are more concerned with nutrition than with taste. The caraway seeds reduce the flatulence that so often results from eating cabbage.

White cabbage, like all cabbages, is medicinal. Whether raw, cooked, or disguised as sauerkraut, many people, including scientists, believe that cabbage decreases the probability of cancer, especially intestinal cancer.

Raw cabbage juice is also thought to have an extraordinary healing effect on ulcers. Some believe that if you drink one cup of freshly-extracted white cabbage juice daily, you will probably be rid of your ulcer in about three weeks.

Cabbage has also been credited with strengthening the immune system and destroying bacteria and viruses.

Salad-e-Sabzi

❧

"Even fossils embedded in stone dream of fresh herbs."
This Persian proverb, and the word sabzi, meaning greens and herbs,
inspired me to create the following recipe.

❧

1 head iceberg lettuce, coarsely sliced

½ bunch Italian parsley, stems removed

½ bunch mint, stems removed

½ bunch chervil, stems removed

1 bunch watercress, stems removed

1 bunch radishes, sliced

1 small cucumber, diced

3 tomatoes, diced

2 scallions, thinly sliced, or 1 red onion, halved and thinly sliced.

A few tbs. of gomasio
(9 parts ground, roasted sesame seeds and 1 part sea salt)

Toss all ingredients and marinate in Vinaigrette Dressing (see page 29).
Sprinkle with a few tablespoons of gomasio.

French Green Bean Salad

❧

*1 lb. or 10 cups green beans,
cleaned, then steamed till they are al dente,
and rinsed with cold water to preserve the color*

4 tomatoes, diced

10 green olives, pitted and sliced

1 tbs. minced parsley

1 tbs. minced chives

1 tbs. minced dill

*1 chili pepper minced,
with or without seeds depending on taste*

Toss these ingredients and set aside. Then prepare the dressing.

❧

DRESSING:

½ cup cold-pressed olive oil

¼ cup balsamic vinegar

1 tbs. Dijon mustard

A touch of garlic

Herb salt, to taste

*Freshly ground pepper,
to taste*

Slivered almonds

For dressing, combine olive oil, vinegar, mustard, garlic, salt, and pepper. Marinate the salad in the dressing. Decorate with a handful of slivered almonds.

BROCCOLI AND BEAN SPROUT SALAD

1 lb. or 5 cups broccoli florets,
raw or steamed al dente

½ lb. or 2 cups bean sprouts

1 red bell pepper, diced

Toss and marinate salad in Gourmet's Garden Dressing (see page 32) or any other dressing.

Borani Esfanaj

❧

This salad is a delicacy from the southern coast of the Caspian Sea,
north of Iran. There rice and tea flourish in terraced beds,
and spinach and mint grow like weeds.

❧

5 oz. plain yogurt

2 small onions, minced

2 tbs. cold-pressed vegetable oil

1 clove garlic, minced

*1 lb. or 16 cups spinach, sorted,
washed, and, if necessary, cut
into smaller pieces*

Herb salt, to taste

Pepper, to taste

¼ bunch mint

*1 tsp. clarified butter
(see Uncommon Ingredients
for preparation)*

½ tsp. turmeric powder

Let yogurt drip through several thicknesses of cheesecloth or a very fine
sieve for 2–3 hours or overnight.

Fry onions in oil until they begin to brown. Add garlic.

After 30 seconds, add spinach and stir-fry briefly, just long enough to
soften the leaves. Transfer the spinach immediately to a bowl to cool.

When it has cooled, stir in salt, pepper, mint, and yogurt very gently.
You don't want a mush. Heat butter in a small pan, add turmeric powder,
and add this mixture to the salad.

Spinach Salad
with
Japanese Plum Wine

❦

½ cup sunflower seeds

1 tbs. sunflower seed oil

½ clove garlic, minced

1 lb. or 16 cups spinach,
sorted, washed, and, if necessary,
cut into small pieces

Pepper, to taste

1 tbs. Japanese plum wine, or to taste

Lemon juice, to taste

Roast sunflower seeds lightly in a dry pan. Add oil and garlic, and finally the spinach. Fry only until it softens. (This happens very fast.)

Transfer the spinach to a bowl, and season with pepper, one or more tablespoons of Japanese plum wine, and lemon juice. Serve immediately.

This is a marvelous hors d'oeuvre from the former Keyno Restaurant in Munich.

BANGKOK VEGETABLE SALAD

❦

½ lb. or 1 ½ cups broccoli or cauliflower florets,
raw or steamed al dente

¼ lb. or 1 ½ cups okra,
cut into two or three pieces, sautéed briefly or raw

2 carrots cut into pieces lengthwise, raw, or steamed al dente

1 red bell pepper, diced

1 yellow bell pepper, diced

1 cup green peas, fresh or frozen

Toss all ingredients. Marinate in Thai Dressing (see page 38). Garnish with tomato wedges and lemon slices.

Thai cuisine is light, particularly the vegetarian dishes. If you do not have one of the vegetables called for in this recipe, don't worry. Improvise freely. The main thing is to capture the distinctive Thai flavor in the dressing.

CHINESE MARINATED EGGPLANT

❦

This salad is typical of Chinese cuisine. Some of our customers in Gourmet's Garden are addicted to it and order it ahead of time.

❦

Peel 1 lb. eggplant and quarter it lengthwise. Steam in a large pot on a rack over boiling water until soft.

Cut eggplant into ¼ inch thick strips and marinate for several hours in Chinese Dressing (see page 37). Sprinkle with sesame seeds.

EGGPLANT ROLLS WITH HERBED QUARK
and
FRESH TOMATO SAUCE

🌿

1 lb. or 5 cups eggplant

1 cup herbed quark

Various mixed garden herbs, minced

Pepper, to taste

Herb salt, to taste

1 bunch basil

Cut eggplant lengthwise into slices ½ inch thick. Bake on a greased cookie sheet in a 375° F oven until soft and let cool.

In the meantime, stir minced herbs into the quark and season with salt and pepper. Put 1–2 tablespoons of quark on each cooled eggplant slice, and roll it up. Place eggplant rolls on their sides in a shallow baking dish on their side.

Serve with warm tomato sauce as a cold appetizer, or serve warm as the main dish. Garnish each eggplant roll with a basil leaf.

For a truly delicious taste, place a small slice of mozzarella cheese under each basil leaf.

Eggplant rolls make very good hors d'oeuvres.

Ali Baba's Root Salad

❦

1–2 tubers fennel,
raw or steamed till al dente
and cut into bite-size pieces

2–4 parsnips or parsley roots
steamed until tender and cut into
bite-size pieces or coarsely grated

2–4 carrots, steamed until tender,
cut into bite-size pieces or coarsely grated

Mix all ingredients and marinate them in Gourmet Dressing (see page 34). Garnish the salad with lovage. You'll love it.

You can also serve this with tomato sauce as a warm dish.

Indian Kohlrabi Salad

❦

½ lb. or 1½ cups young, delicate kohlrabi,
coarsely grated or steamed al dente
and cut into bite-size pieces

½ lb. or 2 cups young, delicate carrots,
coarsely grated or steamed al dente
and cut into bite-size pieces

Mix vegetables and marinate in Indian Dressing (see page 36). Garnish with fresh coriander or parsley.

For a variation on this salad, substitute celery for kohlrabi.

Yucatán Bean Salad

1 cup red kidney beans

1 red onion, thinly sliced into rings

¼ cup pitted green olives, coarsely chopped

2 tomatoes cut into small pieces

1 small cucumber, diced

1 yellow bell pepper, diced

½ cup kernels sweet corn, fresh or frozen

Small slice feta cheese, 3 oz. (optional)

2 hard boiled eggs, chopped (optional)

Soak red kidney beans overnight, and then boil until tender. Cool beans slowly in the cooking water so that they do not burst. Discard cooking water.

Mix all salad ingredients and marinate them in your version of Free-style Pesto (see page 39).

If you like, you can add a small slice (3 oz.) of feta cheese or two chopped, hard-boiled eggs to the salad.

VEGETABLE DISHES

and

SAUCES

VEGETABLE DISHES AND SAUCES

❦

MOST PEOPLE LOVE SAUCES. Occasionally we serve a sauceless dish at Gourmet's Garden, and when we do, some customers are sure to ask for a sauce. It is not our intention to cover every dish with a sauce, or to denigrate sauces to a mere means of making food slide down more easily. No! A good sauce has a nobler raison d'être. Sauces help distribute spices evenly over vegetables or grains, and unite ingredients harmoniously. When they are carefully prepared with fresh ingredients, good sauces are also nourishing. This is not so with instant or semi-prepared sauces or those served in most restaurants. These sauces are a triumph of chemical laboratories where convenience products are the order of the day.

SAUCES COMPLEMENT

A good sauce should complement food, not hide it. If your vegetables are drowning in butter sauce, or your spaghetti in tomato sauce, send them back. You deserve better. A sauce should be creamy, thick enough to just coat your food. Cookbooks tell you to add wine or water to meat juices, and then thicken them with flour. Italians prefer to cook their tomato sauces a long time to thicken them. We, of course, don't like thickening or long cooking. For one thing, they're too time-consuming. For another, long cooking destroys nutrients and can create new, harmful substances.

The sauces we suggest are easy to prepare and easy to digest. No thick béchamel sauces or heavy cheese sauces for us. You will have to go to other cookbooks for those recipes. We intend to give the vegetables center stage, not the sauces!

THICK SAUCES

Preparing a *roux* is the classic method of thickening a sauce with flour. If you must use flour for thickening, try sprinkling a small amount of whole grain flour through a flour sifter over the sauce, stir it, and bring the sauce briefly to a boil. You can also knead butter and finely ground whole grain flour together, shape little dumplings, and add them to your sauce to thicken it. The sauce will not be lumpy. You do have to bring the sauce briefly to a boil to make sure the flour is dissolved in the liquid and you don't taste it. You can make the dumplings ahead of time and keep them in the refrigerator.

Finely ground Japanese kudzu and arrowroot are also good thickening agents. We do not recommend using starch (such as cornstarch) or tomato paste because they are very acidic.

For lighter, better, more delicious thick sauces try the following:

- Sauté plenty of chopped onions. When they begin to brown, add water and continue to cook until they are soft. Mash with a potato masher and you have a nice, thick sauce.

- Cook and purée vegetables, especially root vegetables such as carrots, parsnips, parsley roots, celery, and, of course, potatoes, to create another good thickener.

- Puréed apples are good thickeners for curry dishes.

- Peanuts, almonds, and other kinds of puréed nuts also work well as thickeners.

- From India, we have learned that we can also thicken sauces with puréed lentils, peas, or beans. These dishes are called *dhansak*.

- Most of all, cream is a real blessing in sauces. We prefer sweet cream. If you want to avoid dairy products, we recommend thickened coconut milk, which can be found in Southeast Asian markets and in some supermarkets. Thickened coconut milk makes delightfully aromatic sauces. As a substitute, thin coconut milk is available canned, or, if you prefer, you can make it yourself. Blanch shredded coconut meat in boiling water and squeeze it dry in a dishcloth. Unfortunately, it won't be the best consistency, which is very thick.

Onions and Vegetable Broths Contribute Flavor

You'll notice that many of the recipes that follow begin with browned onions. Searing improves flavor. However, if you want to avoid onions because they don't agree with you, or fried foods because you don't want to eat heated fat, you can manage without them.[3] Just steam your vegetables and add a sauce.

Unlike meat, vegetables do not produce juices to flavor sauces. Some books recommend boiling down leftover vegetables and using the stock or vegetable broth as the basis of your sauce. In today's households, where meals are cooked on the run, this is too time-consuming. So go ahead and use granulated vegetable broth or vegetable bouillon cubes. Keep in mind, however, that many of these cubes or granules contain artificial flavorings. Some are a product of food industry laboratories, and they contain traces of carcinogenic substances that don't belong in a healthy diet. Read the labels carefully. Many of these products also contain yeast. People who suffer from intestinal yeast infections must avoid yeast, although yeast flakes sprinkled on food or added to sauces to enhance flavor are fine for healthy people and should not be condemned across the board. Yeast contains many beneficial ingredients, including vitamin B-complex.

---

3. Heated fat is always more difficult to digest than cold fat. The higher the temperature, and the longer the frying process, the more harmful the fat. This is why fat used for deep-fat frying is so hard on the body. Fat should never be heated to the point where it begins to destabilize and smoke. When this happens throw the fat away, clean the pan, and start over. Coconut oil is the most stable when heated.

SOY SAUCE: JAPANESE SOY SAUCE AND TAMARI

Soy sauce is a good seasoning but is very salty, so use it carefully. Japanese soy sauce contains fermented soy beans and wheat. Tamari tastes even better and consists only of soy beans. Buy only good quality soy sauce that is naturally brewed. Inexpensive soy sauce has many chemicals, and it is not prepared and ripened naturally.

MONOSODIUM GLUTAMATE

Indonesian, Thai, Chinese, and Japanese cuisines often use monosodium glutamate, a flavor intensifier. This chemical produces the desired result, but leaves some people with so-called Chinese restaurant syndrome, causing hours of unpleasant symptoms such as rapid heart beat, dizziness, hot flashes and nausea—or sometimes just a sleepless night. MSG is also found in many instant, prepared, and semi-prepared foods. The processed food industry cannot do without it because the natural flavors of the ingredients have been greatly diminished by processing. Needless to say, you should avoid MSG.

And now for the vegetable dishes...

Mediterranean Vegetables
with
Oven Roasted Potatoes

❧

Imagine a simple but delicious meal with a dark red wine in a little garden restaurant, late at night with a southerly breeze. The following recipe will help you recreate this fantasy on your own patio. Invite a few friends and prepare the meal ahead of time. Guests can help themselves. Serve with a colorful leaf lettuce and cucumbers, tomatoes, and Italian Dressing (see pages 30).

❧

1 medium zucchini, sliced

1 medium eggplant, sliced

1 red bell pepper,
cut in broad strips

1 green bell pepper,
cut in broad strips

1 yellow bell pepper,
cut in broad strips

½ lb. or 3 cups medium
mushrooms

10 medium potatoes,
scrubbed, sliced in half
lengthwise and notched crosswise

Olive oil

Herb salt, to taste

Pepper, to taste

Oregano, to taste

Cumin, to taste

Caraway seed, to taste

Olives, any type, pitted

Basil leaves, to taste

Spread zucchini, eggplant, bell peppers, mushrooms, and potatoes on an oiled baking sheet, brush with olive oil, and roast at 375° F for 30 to 40 minutes.

Potatoes need longer to cook so start them 15 minutes before the other vegetables. When the vegetables are done, sprinkle with salt and pepper. Then season the zucchini with oregano, the eggplant with cumin, and the potatoes with caraway seeds.

Arrange the potatoes on a platter surrounded by other vegetables. Garnish with olives and basil leaves. Serve with olive oil and butter if the dish is too dry.

GREEN BEANS PROVENÇAL
and
OTHER VEGETABLES

We first ate this dish with farmers we met in Provence, France near a city called Castellane. Here in this heavenly place, scented with lavender, they still know how to cook a wonderful meal using the most simple ingredients, and they know the importance of eating and digesting slowly and leisurely. After all, it's not only what you eat, but how you eat it.

1 medium onion, minced (optional)

1 lb. or 5 cups green beans, washed and broken into pieces

1 tbs. olive oil or clarified butter (see Uncommon Ingredients for preparation)

1 red bell pepper, diced

1 yellow bell pepper, diced

¼ to ⅓ cup water

½ lb. or 1 cup tomatoes (preferably plum tomatoes), diced

1 tsp. granulated vegetable bouillon

½ tsp. dried basil or a few sprigs of fresh basil, minced

½ tsp. dried savory, or a few sprigs fresh savory, minced

Herb salt, to taste

Freshly ground pepper, to taste

1 cup sour cream

Fresh herbs for additional seasoning and garnish

Brown the onions in olive oil or clarified butter. Add beans, bell peppers and approximately ¼ to ⅓ of a cup of water. Cover and simmer vegetables over low heat until they are al dente.

Add tomatoes, granulated vegetable bouillon, herbs, and seasonings. Remove pot from heat, and when it has cooled a little, stir in the sour cream, then season and garnish with fresh herbs. Serve at once. (Do not let the sour cream boil or it will curdle.)

RUSTIC RED BEET FEAST

❦

This simple, rustic, earthy dish brings to mind scrubbed wooden
tables, long benches, stone walls, earthenware jugs filled
with cider, and a shepherd asleep by an open fire.
It is a treat for all who like good, solid food.

❦

*8 oz. of onions, coarsely
chopped*

¼ cup sesame oil

*1 lb. or 2 cups red beets,
scrubbed and cut into long,
bite-size pieces*

Caraway seeds, to taste

Fennel, to taste

Pepper, to taste

Herb salt, to taste

*Fresh lovage
(or any other garden herb
of your choice) for garnish*

2–3 tbs sour cream

*Gomasio
(9 parts ground sesame seeds
and 1 part sea salt)*

Sauté onions in sesame oil in a wok or a pot until they are transparent.
Add red beets, cover, and braise very slowly over low heat. Stir occasionally until beets are as soft as you like them.

While beets are cooking, lightly pound caraway and fennel in a mortar.
Add them to the vegetables along with freshly ground pepper.

When the vegetables are done, season with herb salt. Garnish with
lovage and a dollop of sour cream (optional). Have gomasio ready for
those who like it .

Serve beets with soaked buckwheat enriched with butter if desired.

GOURMET'S BROCCOLI

❦

We've cooked this dish at Gourmet's Garden hundreds of times.
We usually add fried, diced tofu. Our customers always
love it as much as we do.

❦

½ lb. or 2 cups onions, coarsely chopped (optional)	1 tsp. granulated vegetable bouillon
¼ cup sunflower seed oil	Herb salt (for light seasoning)
1 red bell pepper, diced	Pepper (for light seasoning)
1 green bell pepper, diced	Turmeric (for light seasoning)
1 yellow bell pepper, diced	Fresh minced herbs (dill, chives, parsley), to taste
2 heads broccoli, florets separated, stems diced	Fresh whole herbs (dill, chives, parsley), for garnish
1¼ cup cream	2 tomatoes, for garnish

Sauté onions (optional) in oil until they are transparent. Add peppers, broccoli, and a little water. Cover and braise slowly over low heat until the vegetables have reached desired softness. Stir occasionally.

Add cream and vegetable bouillon, heat briefly, and season lightly with the three spices.

Put vegetables into a serving bowl, stir in herbs, and garnish with whole herbs and tomatoes cut into quarters or eighths.

Potatoes in their skins are our favorite side dish.

Ragout of Autumn Vegetables

❧

Many people love this dish and find it soothing because it reminds
them of their mother's kitchen. Thanks to the fried onions,
vegetable broth, and the flavor of the root vegetables, the taste
is intense, and even faintly reminiscent of meat dishes.
If you still long for something "meaty" you can slice and sauté
some preserved soy sausage and add it to the ragout.

❧

4 large onions, minced

*¼ cup clarified butter
(see Uncommon Ingredients
for preparation)*

2 cups water

1 lb. or 4 cups carrots, diced

*¼ lb. or 1 cup parsnip
or parsley root, diced*

1 cup green peas, fresh or frozen

¼ cup cream

1 tsp. paprika

Pepper, to taste

Herb salt, to taste

*Fresh chopped herbs
(tarragon, chervil, lovage,
parsley), to taste*

In a big pot or wok, brown the onions in the butter. Add 2 cups of water
and simmer for 10 minutes.

Purée onions. Add root vegetables and cook covered until nearly done.
Toward the end of the cooking time, make sure that more than one half
of the cooking liquid has evaporated. If not, the sauce will be too thin.
(If there's too much liquid at this point, just pour some off. Do not cook
longer or at a higher temperature to get rid of the excess liquid.)

When the vegetables are cooked, add the other ingredients, and season
to taste. Whole-grain noodles or rice are good with this dish, but mashed
potatoes are best.

DELICIOUS KASHMIR VEGETABLES

❦

On one of his many trips, Devanando lived for two weeks on Lake Nagin near Srinagar in Kashmir, in northern India. The expedition's cook regaled the entire group with delicious vegetarian meals around the clock. Devanando took advantage of the opportunity to learn about the Kashmiri art of cooking with spices, and how to harvest vegetables in a boat in a floating garden.

❦

1 large onion, minced

¼ lb. or 1 cup potatoes, finely grated

¼ cup clarified butter (see Uncommon Ingredients, for preparation)

2 cups water

1 tsp. granulated vegetable bouillon

½ tsp. ground cardamom

½ tsp. ground cinnamon

White pepper, to taste

1 pinch of ground cloves

Herb salt, to taste

½ tsp. ground fennel

1 tbs. fresh ginger root, grated

½ lb. carrots, diced

1 fennel root, diced

2 medium zucchini, diced

¼ cup cream

1 bunch fresh coriander leaves (cilantro) or 1–2 sprigs lovage

Sauté onions and potatoes in clarified butter. Stir frequently. Add 2 cups of water, simmer onions and potatoes until done, then purée them.

Add vegetable bouillon, spices, carrots, fennel, and zucchini. Simmer until al dente. Add a little water if needed, depending upon how thick you would like the sauce.

Round the dish off with cream, and season (or garnish) it with herbs. As a side dish we recommend Basmati rice prepared with a little turmeric.

If you do not want onions, or prefer not to eat fried food, you can use ½ pound mashed potatoes as a thickener.

Pea and Mushroom Curry
from
Rajasthan

⚘

Rajasthan is the desert state of northwestern India. It boasts many splendid castles, some of which are famous from old movies. The food there is typically fatty and too spicy, and the original recipe for this curry has no place in this book. So in consideration of your liver, we've drastically reduced the fat and spices. Now you can enjoy the aroma and taste of the magnificent seasonings, which will stimulate your digestion. Dishes from Rajasthan are as colorful as the women's saris. Red tones dominate.

⚘

½ lb. or 2 cups onions, minced

¼ lb. or ½ cup potatoes, coarsely grated

½ cup sesame oil or clarified butter (see Uncommon Ingredients for preparation)

1 chili pepper, seeds removed, minced

1 clove garlic, minced

1 tbs. ginger root, slivered

1 cup water (depending on the consistency and amount of sauce desired)

5 oz. cream

1 tsp. granulated vegetable bouillon

2 tbs. mild curry powder

Freshly ground pepper, to taste

Herb salt, to taste

½ lb. or 3 cups mushrooms, cut into quarters or eighths

2 cups green peas, fresh or frozen

Brown grated potatoes and onions in half the clarified butter or sesame oil. Add chili pepper, garlic, and ginger. Fry for one more minute.

Add water and cream, vegetable bouillon, and all remaining spices. Purée the sauce and season to taste.

In the meantime, sauté mushrooms in remaining clarified butter or sesame oil. When they are done, put them and the peas into the hot sauce. The peas do not need to be cooked.

This dish goes well with rice or millet.

Sautéed Hawaiian White Cabbage

❦

Devanando first tasted this dish on a brief visit to a commune
on the Hawaiian island of Maui. The following recipe is a tropical
variation of our popular and healthful white cabbage. The commune
offered a tremendous variety of foods because every member,
as well as guests, contributed to the menu.

❦

*1 large onion,
coarsely chopped (optional)*

¼ cup sunflower seed oil

*1 lb. or 4 cups white cabbage,
coarsely sliced*

1 cup water

5 oz. coconut cream

1 tsp. ground cumin

1 tsp. ground coriander

1 tsp. ground fennel

1 tsp. ground turmeric

½ cup sour cream

*1 tsp. granulated vegetable
bouillon*

*Freshly ground pepper,
to taste*

Herb salt, to taste

3 tsp. coconut flakes

1 tomato

Sauté onions in oil until they are transparent. Add white cabbage and
continue to sauté, stirring occasionally. Finally add water, cover, and
simmer until done.

Add the other ingredients and season to taste. The dish should not be
too moist, but somewhat dry. (Some of the water will evaporate.)
Garnish with coconut flakes and tomato wedges.

Serve with baked sweet potatoes or brown rice.

Guacamole and Potatoes in their Skins

❦

Guacamole is a Mexican avocado purée. This is our favorite
(low-fat) version. If you want to prepare it in authentic Mexican style,
you must add garlic, a minced onion, and lots of chili pepper.
Mexicans don't usually eat guacamole with potatoes,
but we think the two are a delightful combination.

❦

10 to 15 medium-size potatoes

*3 soft avocados,
peeled with pit removed*

*2 plum tomatoes or 1 large
beefsteak tomato, minced*

*½ bunch fresh coriander leaves
(cilantro) or other herbs,
minced*

Freshly ground pepper, to taste

Herb salt, to taste

1 tsp. lemon juice

Boil potatoes in their skins. While potatoes are boiling, mash avocados
and tomatoes with a fork.

When potatoes are done, mix with remaining ingredients and season to
taste. You can also eat the potatoes separately if you wish. You can make
the avocado go further by adding sour cream. Experiment with a variety
of spices.

If you serve guacamole with potatoes or bread, use very little lemon
juice, since acid impedes the digestion of starches. This is a simple,
delicious, and healthful dish that can be prepared very quickly. Serve it
with the tender inner leaves of romaine lettuce.

VEGETABLES WITH CEYLONESE GINGER
and
COCONUT SAUCE

❦

You've probably noticed by now that we are very fond of coconut. If you ever crave something really solid to chew on, buy yourself a fresh coconut and chew the meat. Don't eat too much, though, because coconut is not one of the most digestible foods.

On a trip through the divine tropical island of Ceylon, Devanando noticed that as days went by, more and more people in his group were ordering vegetarian dishes. The vegetarians were feasting on all the glorious native vegetable curries—many served with coconut sauces—while the meat-eaters got grumpier and grumpier as they gnawed meats prepared English-style; that is, cooked to the consistency of a tough old rag. Unfortunately, even the large hotels in Ceylon serve mostly what they call "international cuisine." The magic of the tropical native kitchen can only be found in the traditional inns and small hotels that survived British rule.

❦

½ lb. or 2 cups Brussels sprouts, cleaned, and cut in half, or bell peppers, diced

¼ cup sesame oil or clarified butter (see Uncommon Ingredients for preparation)

½ lb. or 2 cups carrots, cut into julienne strips

½ lb. zucchini, cut into julienne strips

SAUCE:

1 tbs. fresh ginger root, minced

2 cups water

3 stalks lemon grass,
thinly sliced on the diagonal
(or substitute grated lemon
peel, measured to taste)

1 tsp. granulated vegetable
bouillon

1 bunch fresh mint, minced

½ tsp. minced galagan
or galagan powder

5 oz. coconut cream

½ tsp. minced turmeric
or turmeric powder

Freshly ground pepper, to taste

Herb salt, to taste

1 tomato, diced

Put Brussels sprouts or peppers, and carrots, in a wok or covered pot.
Braise over low heat in butter or oil until vegetables are al dente.
Stir occasionally. A little water will speed up this process. About halfway
through the cooking time (5 to 7 minutes) add zucchini.

In the meantime, heat water and spices for the sauce, and simmer for a
few minutes so that the spices impart flavor to the water.

Remove the slices of lemon grass and discard. Add the rest of the ingredients, remove wok from heat, and season to taste.

Place vegetables in a serving bowl and add sauce. Garnish with fresh
mint leaves and pieces of tomato. Serve with fresh chutney, also called
sambal (see page 40) and Basmati rice.

If you choose this dish for the protein-based menu on page 17, serve it
without rice and substitute fried tempeh chips (thin, oval tempeh slices,
seasoned with salt and pepper, and moistened with coconut sauce).

Delicious Fresh Garden Vegetables

꩜

You can make this quick, simple, delicious dish in no time at all.
The ingredients are easy to find. You could serve this dish with
Veggie Burgers (see page 132) or with a tempeh or tofu cutlet.

꩜

*½ lb. or 1½ cups kohlrabi,
thinly sliced*

½ lb. or 1½ cups carrots, sliced

*½ lb. or 5 cups green beans,
broken in half*

*¼ cup clarified butter
(see Uncommon Ingredients
for preparation)*

Freshly ground pepper, to taste

Herb salt, to taste

A few sprigs savory, minced

Braise vegetables, covered, in clarified butter. Stir occasionally.

When the vegetables are crisp-tender or soft, season them with pepper,
salt, and minced savory or other garden herbs.

This dish is delicious, and filling all by itself.

EGGPLANT KURMA
from the
IMPERIAL MOGUL KITCHEN

❦

Kurma are dishes that were prepared for Mogul emperors.
They are enriched and thickened with nuts and are considered
particularly refined and elegant. You can, of course, use other
vegetables in addition to eggplant. To learn more about the
glories of the Mogul Empire without traveling to India, study the
Indian miniatures you see in Indian restaurants, markets,
and books. These people lived an elegant life devoted to
celebrating the senses, a life of affluence and beauty.

❦

1 medium onion, minced

*¼ cup sesame oil
or clarified butter
(see Uncommon Ingredients
for preparation of clarified
butter)*

*1 clove garlic, chopped
(optional)*

1 tbs. freshly grated ginger

¼ tsp. ground coriander

¼ tsp. ground fennel

¼ tsp. ground cumin

¼ tsp. ground turmeric

¼ tsp. ground paprika

*1 tsp. granulated vegetable
broth dissolved in 1 cup water*

*1 lb. or 5 cups eggplant,
diced*

2 cups water

*5 oz. almond purée,
stirred into 1 cup of water*

Herb salt, to taste

Pepper, to taste

½ cup peas, fresh or frozen

*2 tbs. fresh coriander leaves
(cilantro), part of it minced*

1 cup slivered almonds

Brown onions in oil. Add garlic, ginger, and spices. Sauté for one minute, stirring constantly.

Add vegetable broth and eggplant, stir well, and cook until soft.

Finally, add the two cups of water and almond purée, season with pepper and herb salt, and at the end, add the peas and minced coriander.

Spoon into a serving bowl. Garnish with coriander leaves and slivered almonds, and serve with millet, rice or chapatti (thin, unleavened Indian bread).

For variety, substitute ½ teaspoon powdered cloves for the cumin, turmeric, and paprika. And use 2 ½ cups plain yogurt instead of the two cups of water and the puréed almonds. Cook the eggplant in the yogurt until done.

Coconut and Thai Vegetables from the Wok

Many years ago Devanando and I traveled in a chauffeured rental car
through Thailand. The chauffeur showed us clean and reasonable
places to spend the night and helped us find good restaurants
and food. We admire Thai cuisine because the dishes are
prepared from fresh ingredients in front of the guests.
Vegetables are almost always al dente, and there is a
great variety of vegetables, herbs, and spices. Thai dishes
are easy to prepare. Thai cuisine differs from Chinese,
but both make skillful use of the wok.

¼ cup vegetable oil

*2 tbs. fresh ginger root,
slivered*

*1 chili pepper minced,
with or without seeds,
depending on how hot
you like it*

*½ lb. or 2½ cups green aspara-
gus, cut on the diagonal into
bite-size pieces*

1 leek, thinly sliced

1 carrot, julienned

*½ lb. or 3 cups snow peas,
cut on the diagonal
into bite-size pieces*

*1 yellow bell pepper,
cut into bite-size pieces*

*1 red bell pepper,
cut into bite-size pieces*

1 cup water

*1 tsp. granulated vegetable
bouillon*

3 oz. coconut cream

*5 lemon leaves,
sliced very fine,
or 1 tbs. grated lemon peel*

Herb salt, to taste

Freshly ground pepper, to taste

Lemon juice, to taste

Heat oil in the wok, and sauté ginger and chili approximately 1 minute.

Add vegetables and stir-fry over highest possible heat until they are soft enough for your taste.

Add water, bouillon, coconut cream, and lemon leaves. Stir well so that the coconut cream melts. Season with salt and pepper and a little lemon juice.

We prefer to eat this dish by itself, without side dishes. The success of this and the next recipe depends a lot on slicing the vegetables so that they look attractive.

Stir-fried Chinese Vegetables

᷿

This is another recipe which takes no time at all to prepare, and,
though it is a cooked dish, it retains large amounts of important
nutrients. It is especially suited for a gathering of friends
around the wok. The best vegetables for this are those that
merely need warming rather than cooking. Tougher
vegetables must be very thinly sliced. Remember, too, that an
ordinary wok can accommodate only two, at most three, portions.
Otherwise the cooking process takes too long and the stir-fried
flavor does not develop. Vegetables will be limp instead of crisp.

᷿

¼ cup sesame oil

1 tbs. ginger root, slivered

1 minced chili pepper
(optional, with or without
seeds, depending on how hot
you like it)

1 clove garlic, minced
(optional)

2 scallions, minced

¼ lb. or 2½ cups fresh shiitake
or oyster mushrooms,
sliced into thin strips

1 leek, sliced diagonally

1 medium Chinese cabbage

¾ cup mung bean sprouts
or lentil sprouts

3 tomatoes,
diced into medium-size pieces

1–2 tbs. Japanese plum wine
(or to taste)

1–2 tbs. tamari, (or to taste)

1–2 tbs. gomasio, or to taste
(to prepare gomasio, combine
9 parts ground sesame
seeds with 1 part sea salt)

Variety of fresh herbs,
minced, to taste

Heat oil in the wok and sauté ginger, chili pepper (optional), garlic, and scallions for 2 minutes. Add mushrooms, and sauté another 2 minutes. Add leek and hard stems of Chinese cabbage, cut into julienne strips.

Sauté 2 more minutes. Then add the tender part of the Chinese cabbage (cut into strips) and sprouts. Stir-fry another 2 minutes at full heat.

Finally add tomatoes, remove the wok from heat, and add Japanese plum wine, tamari, and gomasio. Serve immediately.

Sprinkle each portion with freshly chopped herbs.

Chinese rice is good with this dish, or wheat noodles cooked in water and stirred into the vegetables.

Fresh Tomato Sauce

½ lb. or 2 cups onions, minced

¼ cup butter

1 ¼ cups cream

1 heaping tsp. granulated vegetable bouillon

1 lb. or 2 cups tomatoes, diced

1 bunch basil or parsley, minced

Herb salt, to taste, (optional)

Freshly ground pepper, to taste, (optional)

Brown onions in butter. Add cream and vegetable bouillon and bring to a boil. Remove pot from heat, and add tomatoes and herbs.

Season with salt and pepper. Serve immediately.

This delicious sauce goes extremely well with cooked vegetables.

GRAIN DISHES

GRAIN DISHES

I N THIS BOOK we are emphasizing a diet consisting primarily of fruits, salads, and vegetables, augmented by nuts, seeds and grains. We prefer grain as a side dish, at most served once a day, preferably less often. Grain supplies energy, satisfies hunger, and promotes a feeling of well-being, but it is not the most important food for essential nutrients. Even when eaten sparingly, grain dishes should be cooked properly, so they are easy to digest.

COOKING RICE

Brown Rice

Macrobiotic cooks insist that brown rice must be cooked in a pressure cooker so that the rice will be completely broken down. We suggest you try it once and see whether you like it and whether it agrees with you. Use 2 cups of rice to 1¼ – 1½ cups of water. Rinse the rice well, drain and put it in the pressure cooker. Add water and soak for 2–3 hours. Then heat slowly. When the water boils, add a pinch of salt and close the pot. When the pressure has risen, reduce the heat so that the pressure remains even. Cook for 50 minutes. Remove the pot from the heat and let it stand until the pressure goes down.

We don't want to dictate to you, but we never cook rice in a pressure cooker. We believe, along with many nutritionists, that food prepared in a pressure cooker is exposed to unnecessarily high temperatures. Avoid high temperatures because they create new chemical combinations that we feel may be harmful. We do not recommend preparing vegetables in a pressure cooker either because even expert cooks can't tell when vegetables prepared this way are done, and they often come out mushy and ruined. In addition, they lose too many nutrients, if not all, when cooked for a long time.

Cooking Rice in an Ordinary Pot

Rice cooked in an ordinary pot requires more water, since some will evaporate. The rule of thumb is 1 cup of rice to 1 cup of water and a pinch of salt. Bring the water to a boil, reduce the heat to very low, and let the water simmer for at most one hour, until the rice has absorbed it completely.

Rice prepared this way is heavily saturated and not everyone likes it. Brown rice should be al dente after 30 to 40 minutes, and many people prefer it this way. If the rice is too moist, dry it out in a skillet, stirring constantly, or put it in a casserole and bake it dry in a 200-250° F oven. If, on the other hand, the rice is already dry, but not yet soft enough, you can always add water.

Wonderful Basmati Rice

Basmati rice from India and Pakistan has an incomparable flavor and aroma. When we prepare it, we add enough water to bring the water level to an inch above the rice. We bring the water to a boil and decrease the heat to very low. After 10 to 15 minutes we check the rice, adding water if necessary. Basmati rice takes only 20 to 30 minutes to cook. For small quantities (three servings or so) use a wooden spatula to scrape the rice from the bottom of the pan. If it dries out and sticks, just add a little more water.

There is no perfect recipe for rice. You will always have to judge for yourself, depending on the conditions in your kitchen (oven, pot, thickness of the lid) and the type of grain. If you lower the heat as soon as the water comes to a boil, there is little chance that the rice will burn. We like rice that is light, fluffy, grainy and dry, and slightly al dente. Devanando acquired a taste for rice like this in Persia, where they are experts at preparing *Dom-Siah*, a rice native to the Caspian lowlands. In India they sometimes add about ¼ teaspoon turmeric per cup to the cooking water. This dyes rice a splendid yellow. A little oil and salt, or granulated vegetable bouillon, enhances the taste and aroma.

Cooking Millet

Millet is unjustly neglected here and in other countries. In India, for example, any self-respecting person who can afford it will eat rice or unleavened wheat bread (chapatti) instead. But millet is a grain which tastes good and is not acid forming. It is high in silicon (necessary for skin, hair, and nail growth), and is also good for the stomach, spleen, and pancreas.

The ratio of water to millet should be approximately 1 to 1¼. Millet tends to be bitter. We recommend rinsing it in very hot water before cooking. After rinsing, dry millet for about 5 minutes on an ungreased skillet, though this step is not absolutely necessary.

Put millet and water in a pot, bring to a boil, and decrease heat to very low. Cover. The millet will be ready in 30 minutes. When cooking large amounts, it is advisable to bring the water to a boil first, and then add the millet. To enhance flavor, add a coarsely chopped fried onion to the pot. If you are just having plain millet, add a little oil and salt or granulated vegetable bouillon.

Wheat and Spelt

Prepare wheat and spelt the same way you prepare brown rice. To decrease cooking time, soak grains for at least several hours or overnight. If you are not using a pressure cooker, we recommend equal amounts of water and soaked grain. Check often while cooking to make sure it does not burn. The grains should be tender but not mushy. Try a combination of 1 part spelt, 3 parts rice, and 1 part adzuki beans. Soak the mixture overnight and discard the water. Cook with a little salt, and season with fresh minced dill and roasted sesame oil. Try wheat and spelt sprouts sprinkled over a salad. They sprout in only two to three days.

SOAKING BULGUR

Bulgur is popular in the Balkans, the Near East, the Middle East, and North America. To prepare, soak whole grains in hot water. This drives the vitamins, protein, and minerals from the outer layer of the grains to the center. Then boil the bulgur. The starch seals vitamins and nutrients inside the grain, and turns it into a sticky mass. Then dry the wheat, rub the skin off, sift, and chop coarsely. This entire procedure makes starch more digestible.

Bulgur is quick and easy to prepare since you only have to combine it with 2 to 2½ parts water to 1 part grain, bring to a boil, and let it steep a mere 10 minutes or so. That's all! Bulgur should be dry and fluffy. It is very good with vegetable dishes or served cold as a salad, to which you can add soft vegetables such as tomatoes, cucumbers, bell peppers, zucchini, olives, all kinds of herbs, salt, pepper, and oil. You do not need to cook bulgar if you intend to use it as a salad. Simply soak it overnight.

Couscous, common in Tunisia and other North African countries, is a smaller version of bulgur.

PORRIDGE

Because oats contain 7% fat, they are especially warming and fortifying, and are particularly beneficial in the winter. You can eat oats for lunch or dinner in the form of a porridge made from rolled or whole-grain oats. Use three times as much water as oats, and season with cinnamon, cardamom, and sweet cream.

If you prefer not to cook the oats, soak them for at least 4 hours (better yet, overnight), add a few pitted dates, and purée with a handful of soaked cashews. Season as above. Eat only small portions because this is not an ideal combination.

BUCKWHEAT AND BUCKWHEAT NOODLES

Buckwheat comes from the steppes of southern Russia and was introduced to Europe in the Middle Ages. It can be eaten as a whole grain or groats. Toasted, it is called kasha, which has an especially hearty flavor. In Japan, buckwheat noodles (soba) have been popular for centuries. Most health food stores sell buckwheat in a variety of forms. Since buckwheat does not contain gluten, it is a good choice for people who are allergic to gluten, or those who suffer from wheat allergies or celiac disease.

To cook buckwheat, use twice as much water as grain. Buckwheat requires only a short cooking time and, like millet, is not acid-forming. We recommend it as a supplement to a raw food diet, perhaps with millet and other grains for variety, but for no more than one meal a day. You can also use buckwheat flour for pancakes.

AZTEC GRAIN — AMARANTH

Before Columbus discovered America, amaranth was the staple food of the Aztecs in Central America. Like buckwheat and quinoa, it is not a true grain. It is extraordinarily high in protein (16%) and rich in valuable nutrients. Amaranth does not contain gluten.

You can soak the whole grain, use it as flour for unleavened flatbread, or combine it with spelt to bake rolls. You can also use amaranth for pancakes. Amaranth is most popular as a dessert. The Aztecs prepared a mixture of puffed amaranth and honey, known as *Alegria*. (See page 101 for another dessert using puffed amaranth.). Puffed amaranth is commercially available.

INCAN GRAIN — QUINOA

In the highlands of the South American Andes, the Incas raised quinoa as long ago as three thousand years before Christ. It disappeared during the Spanish conquest and has only recently been cultivated again. Quinoa is a member of the goosefoot family. Like amaranth, it is 16%

protein. Its notable compounds of amino acids put its nutritional value near that of powdered milk. The fat content (7%) is equal to that of oats.

Always wash quinoa thoroughly before using it. After washing, soak it overnight, and rinse it twice again the next day. By evening you will be able to see sprouts, and the sprouted grain will be ready to eat. The grain takes only 15 minutes to cook. It does not get sticky and has a pleasant, light taste. You can use it for salad, as in Quinoa Mexicana or Quinoa Sprouts Mexicana (see page 110).

And now to recipes using grain...

Punjabi Millet and Vegetables

❦

This wonderful, satisfying dish comes from the Land of Five Rivers in the northwestern part of the Indian subcontinent. It combines the nutty taste of millet, the creamy consistency of cooked red lentils, and the crisp texture of vegetables, all wreathed in the aroma of exotic spices. This dish warms and satisfies. We like to serve it on a bed of sliced, raw Chinese cabbage.

❦

1 large onion, diced

2 oz. vegetable oil or clarified butter (see Uncommon Ingredients, for preparation)

½ lb. or 1 cup millet

¼ cup red lentils

1 tsp. granulated vegetable bouillon

2 tsp. mild curry powder

1 tsp. curry leaves or fenugreek leaves crumbled, or a stalk of fresh lovage, minced

6 cardamom seeds, pounded open in a mortar

Herb salt, to taste

Freshly ground pepper, to taste

2 cups water

2 carrots, diced

2 parsnips, diced

1 red bell pepper, diced

1 green bell pepper, diced

½ cup green peas, fresh or frozen

1 tbs. slivered fresh ginger

Chinese cabbage, sliced

In a large pot, sauté the onion in oil or clarified butter.

Rinse the millet with very hot water, and add to onion. Then add all ingredients listed above up to and including salt and pepper.

Add the two cups of water and bring the millet to a boil. Simmer it over low heat for about 10 minutes. Add carrots and parsnips. Cook for another 10 minutes. Add diced peppers. Cook another 10 minutes or until done. If it looks too dry, add a little water.

Before serving, stir in peas and ginger, and season to taste. Serve each portion on a bed of sliced Chinese cabbage.

MOGUL VEGETABLE BIRYANI

🍃

Biryani is a classic dish from northern India. It has a wonderful
flavor and a fluffy, grainy consistency. Classic biryani is prepared
with mutton, but vegetable biryani is equally delicious. If you don't
want to bother with the long list of required spices, find an Indian or
Asian market which sells biryani paste. This is not exactly the same as
the mixture in this recipe, but it is a good substitute. A good biryani is
a dish for special occasions. For those who find this recipe too
complicated, we have added a simpler version.

🍃

1 cup raw or 3 cups
cooked Basmati rice

1 ¼ cups water

½ tsp. turmeric

1 cinnamon stick,
broken into pieces
(or ½ tsp. ground cinnamon)

6 cardamom seeds
pounded open in a mortar

10 whole cloves

¼ tsp. ground coriander

¼ tsp. ground cumin

2 tsp. granulated vegetable
bouillon

Herb salt, to taste

¼ lb. or 2 ½ cups green beans,
cut into small pieces

¼ lb. or 1 cup small
cauliflower florets

¼ lb. or 1 cup carrots, sliced

¼ cup clarified butter
(see Uncommon Ingredients
for preparation)

¼ lb. or 1 cup button mushrooms
or oyster mushrooms, diced

½ cup green peas, fresh or frozen

½ tsp. saffron threads, pulverized
in a small mortar and dissolved
in half a cup of water

2 onions, halved and sliced

1 cup slivered almonds

1 ½ cup cashews,
coarsely chopped

1 tbs. fresh ginger root, slivered

Salt, to taste

½ cup coconut flakes

3 tomatoes,
cut into eight pieces each

Wash rice and roast it in a large skillet until dry. Place in a large pot and add water.

While the water is coming to a boil over high heat, add the first six spices and the vegetable bouillon. When the rice comes to a boil, reduce the heat to very low and cover the pot. Simmer until rice is almost tender. Season with herb salt and keep hot.

In the meantime, braise the beans, cauliflower, and carrots in clarified butter, covered over low heat, stirring occasionally, until they are al dente.

In another pan, fry mushrooms over high heat.

Grease and heat a soufflé mold (with lid). Start with a layer of rice, then a layer of vegetables, mushrooms and peas, and repeat the layering process again. Spread the rest of the rice on top. Finally, sprinkle warm saffron water over the dish and cover tightly with a lid. Place in a 375° F oven and cook until done (about 20 minutes).

In the meantime, fry onions until they are nearly brown, and add almonds, cashews, and ginger. Season with salt. Add coconut flakes and tomatoes. Top soufflé with this mixture.

Serve on a large, pre-warmed serving dish.

In the simplified version, boil rice with a little oil, vegetable bouillon, biryani paste and your favorite vegetables. Add the saffron water shortly before the rice and vegetables are ready. Garnish with fried onions. It's that easy!

Fried Rice with Vegetables and Sprouts

🌾

This is a particularly good way to use leftover rice. It is easy and
quick to prepare, tastes good, and is satisfying. If you always have
leftover rice in the refrigerator, you may easily become addicted
to this dish, because it is so light, easy to cook, and delicious.
Some people add bits of omelet or pieces of roasted meat,
which we do not advocate because this is not a good combination.
If someone in your family still eats meat, and you prefer not
to prepare separate special meals, you could offer this dish.
Fry the egg or the meat separately and mix it with
one serving of the vegetable rice.

🌾

2 onions, minced	½ cup lentil sprouts, chickpea sprouts, or mung bean sprouts (or a combination of all three)
2 oz. vegetable oil	
1 red bell pepper, diced	1 cup cooked rice (made with ½ cup raw rice)
1 leek, sliced	
1–2 zucchini, (depending on size), diced	Freshly ground pepper, to taste
	Herb salt, to taste
1 yellow bell pepper, diced	Lots of minced herbs

In a large skillet or wok, sauté onions in oil, add remaining vegetables,
and sauté (or braise) until they are as soft as you like them.

Add rice, season with salt and pepper, or whatever you like, and heat.
Put the fried rice in a serving bowl.

Garnish with minced herbs. Serve with a lettuce salad.

Kasha with Oyster Mushrooms

❧

We would love to be able to say that we discovered the next recipe
in a peasant's hovel on the steppes of southern Russia.
But, unfortunately, we have never been to Russia.
Instead we offer you the following meal with an Italian flavor.
It is particularly suitable for special occasions.

❧

¼ lb. roasted buckwheat

1 ¼ cups water

1 tsp. granulated vegetable
bouillon, or more to taste

1 onion, minced

2 oz. olive oil plus a dash

½ lb. or 3 ½ cups
oyster mushrooms,
cut into bite-size pieces

Freshly ground pepper, to taste

Herb salt, to taste

¼ lb. or 3 cups arugula,
cut into thin strips

¼ lb. or 3 cups spinach,
cut into thin strips

15 olives, pitted and chopped
(green or black)

Dash of lemon juice

Simmer buckwheat in water, adding bouillon.

In the meantime, sauté onions in olive oil in a large skillet, increase
heat, and add mushrooms. The mushrooms should be fried, not braised.
A high temperature enhances the flavor of the mushrooms. If they
release a lot of moisture, add it to the buckwheat. When the mushrooms
are tender, season them with pepper and herb salt.

Serve as individual portions in the following way: Fill a cup with kasha, and
turn the cup upside down in the middle of the plate. Surround the kasha
with a thick layer of arugula and spinach. Distribute fried mushrooms,
and sprinkle with chopped olives, a dash of olive oil, and lemon juice.

Osaka Spelt

With this recipe we offer a taste of the macrobiotic diet, which includes many beneficial elements. However, we don't recommend a complete macrobiotic diet because so few fresh and raw fruits and vegetables are used.

¼ lb. or ½ cup spelt

Approximately 1 oz. tamari

2 carrots, diced

1 small red beet, diced

½–1 celery root
(depending on size), diced

2 oz. sesame oil

1 leek, sliced

2 oz. edible seaweed
or marine salad[4], soaked and
cut into small pieces

1 tsp. ground coriander

Gomasio (9 parts ground
sesame seed and 1 part sea salt)

½ bunch chives, chopped
for garnish

Olives, chopped, for garnish

Soak spelt in water overnight, and then simmer over low heat in water used for soaking until tender. When spelt is tender, season with tamari.

In the meantime, braise diced root vegetables in sesame oil. You may add a little water to speed the cooking process and prevent sticking. When they are about halfway done, after approximately 7 minutes, add the leek and seaweed or marine salad.

Stir all ingredients together in a large pot, season with coriander and gomasio. Let stand briefly to allow the flavors to blend. Garnish with chopped chives and olives.

4. The edible seaweed must be the kind that is soft after soaking and 7 minutes of cooking. Marine salad is a type of seaweed that is so finely textured you can eat it almost without cooking it.

Quinoa Mexicana
and
Quinoa Sprouts Mexicana

⚘

¼ lb. or ½ cup quinoa
or quinoa sprouts

4 plum tomatoes
or 2 beefsteak tomatoes, diced

1 green bell pepper, diced

1 yellow bell pepper, diced

1 red bell pepper, diced

1 rib celery, diced

2 scallions, minced

½ cup olive oil

2 tbs. lemon juice

Freshly ground pepper,
 to taste

Herb salt, to taste

⅓ cup green olives, chopped

1 bunch fresh coriander
or mint, minced

1 chili pepper, minced

Cook quinoa or sprout it.

To make quinoa sprouts, wash quinoa thoroughly, then soak it overnight. Rinse it twice again the next day, and by evening you will see sprouts, and the sprouted grain will be ready to eat.

In the meantime, cut vegetables and prepare a dressing using remaining ingredients. Finally, toss everything together and leave it in a cool place.

These dishes are ideal for a cold buffet. Try them!

Tabbouleh

&

This bulgur and herb salad is very popular in the Middle East,
especially in Morocco and Egypt. There is only one problem with
tabbouleh. The original recipe calls for the juice of two to three
lemons (or limes), which interferes with the digestion of grains.
We've decreased the number of lemons, but the salad is still excellent.
Tabbouleh is always found on Middle Eastern buffets along with
hummus (see page 155), tahini (see page 33), falafel (see page 134),
baba ghanouj (see page 159), and Salad-e-Sabzi (see page 55).

&

*½ lb. or 1 cup dry bulgur,
soaked in water overnight
(or at least one hour)*

3 scallions, minced

1 bunch parsley, minced

1 bunch mint, minced

3 tbs. cold-pressed olive oil

Herb salt, to taste

Freshly ground pepper, to taste

Romaine lettuce leaves

1 tbs. lemon or lime juice

3 tomatoes, diced

Place bulgur in a fine sieve and squeeze out moisture. Spread grains on a
dishcloth and allow to dry a little more. Then mix the bulgur with scallions, herbs, oil, and spices in a big bowl, or preferably, a tea towel,
muslin or clean cloth.

Serve on romaine lettuce leaves, sprinkle with lemon juice, and garnish
with diced tomatoes.

WHOLE-GRAIN MILLET NOODLES
with
SAGE AND VEGETABLES

❦

½ lb. noodles

1 onion, diced

3 red bell peppers, diced

¼ cup olive oil

½ lb. or 6 cups spinach,
stems removed,
leaves coarsely cut

½ cup sunflower seeds

½ cup cream

3 tbs. fresh sage, minced

Salt, to taste

Freshly ground pepper,
to taste

Parmesan or pecorino
cheese, freshly grated,
for seasoning

Boil noodles in sufficient water with a pinch of salt and oil. Meanwhile, prepare the sauce.

Sauté onion and braise bell pepper in olive oil until they are as tender as you like. Then add the spinach, braising only until it softens. Add sunflower seeds, cream, and sage, and season with salt and pepper. When serving, season each portion with a little freshly grated Parmesan or pecorino cheese.

We don't think adding grated cheese creates a bad combination of ingredients, as long as it is a very small amount and you treat the cheese as you would a spice.

This dish is equally delicious made with semolina spaghetti or fettuccine.

Whole-Grain Spaghetti
with
Mushrooms and Cream Sauce

This is an Italian classic. You'll love it. The peas are optional, but they add color. So do the diced tomatoes you use to decorate each portion. You may be surprised that we don't have a recipe for spaghetti and tomato sauce. As explained earlier, tomatoes are acidic, and acid hinders the digestion of the starch contained in spaghetti.

½ lb. whole-grain spaghetti

¼ cup sunflower oil

1 onion, diced

½ lb. or 3 cups button or other mushrooms, cleaned and cut into pieces

⅔ cup cream

1 tsp. granulated vegetable bouillon

½ cup green peas, fresh or frozen

½ bunch fresh basil, minced

Herb salt, to taste

Freshly ground pepper, to taste

Boil spaghetti in water with a little salt and oil. Meanwhile, prepare the sauce.

In the sunflower oil sauté the onion and braise the mushrooms until they are as soft as you like them. Add cream, vegetable bouillon, peas and basil. Season with salt and pepper.

This dish is especially good made with porcini mushrooms.

Fettuccine with Broccoli Florets

Broccoli has become very popular in recent years. This is good news
because broccoli, like all members of the cabbage family,
contains important nutrients. Another reason we like broccoli
so much is that sauce clings so well to the florets. Eat small florets
of broccoli raw in salads, or, as in this recipe, eat it cooked al dente.

½ lb. fettuccine
(perhaps green fettuccine,
made with spinach)

1 onion, minced

¼ cup sunflower oil

2–4 tbs. of water for braising

½ lb. or 2 ½ cups
broccoli florets

1 red bell pepper, diced

⅔ cup cream

2 tbs. capers, chopped

Paprika, to taste

Herb salt, to taste

Freshly ground pepper, to taste

1 bunch mixed garden herbs,
minced

Boil noodles in plenty of water with a little salt and oil. Meanwhile, prepare the sauce.

Sauté onion in sunflower oil, add 2–4 tablespoons of water, and braise
broccoli florets and pepper until they are just soft enough for you.

Add cream and capers, and season with paprika, salt and pepper. Garnish
each portion with herbs.

CRUNCHY SEITAN

Seitan consists primarily of wheat protein. You can buy it ready-made, or you can make it yourself. To make seitan yourself, combine 4 ½ pounds of finely milled wheat flour (spelt flour makes good seitan) and 4 ¾ cups water, mix and knead. Let the dough stand for at least 15 minutes, then knead vigorously for another 15 minutes.

Place the dough into a large bowl and add water. Let it stand for several hours, then knead the dough in the water. If the dough falls apart, pour the excess water through a sieve and knead the dough in fresh, warm water. This releases the starch, which you discard with every change of water.

After 15 to 20 minutes the seitan will be ready. If you keep on kneading, the protein content of the seitan will increase until there is no starch left at all. Toward the end the water will turn slightly milky.

Boil the seitan in water for 1 hour. Watch at first that it doesn't stick to the pot.

You can slice seitan and sauté it with onions, cut it into thin strips and add a sauce, or add it to vegetables in a wok. Seitan is chewy, very much like meat, and can serve as a substitute for those who are trying to give up eating meat.

Dr. Franz Susman of Ljubliana, in the former Yugoslavia, gave us this recipe.

LEGUMES

LEGUMES

≈

LEGUMES (PEAS, LENTILS, AND BEANS) are high in protein and play an important part in human nutrition. The best way to eat legumes is in the form of sprouts. Since many people find sprouts rather dull, we recommend adding small amounts to other vegetables shortly before serving. Be careful that the sprouts don't get heated unnecessarily, since important nutrients are lost to heat. You can add legume sprouts to other ingredients puréed in a food processor with a chopping blade, or in a juicer.

Legumes are most beneficial when combined with vegetables or salad. Rice and lentils, or corn tortillas with beans, are easy to digest. In India and Mexico they are practically national staples. Like grain, legumes keep well.

SOAK WELL

Legumes have a reputation for causing flatulence in many people. Our bodies do not have enough enzymes to digest certain complex sugars which are found in legumes. Bacteria reduce these undigested sugars in the large intestine and free unwanted gases. The more legumes we eat, the more the body adapts to these sugars and the less gas it produces. To minimize the problem, soak legumes as follows. This process will get rid of 90% of these complex sugars:

Wash legumes thoroughly and discard the water. Then pour boiling water over the legumes and soak for at least four hours (or overnight if possible). For each cup of legumes, add a pinch of baking soda to neutralize it. This will allow the legumes to absorb more water. (This also works for chickpeas, which sprout well after this treatment. Of course, in order to sprout they must be soaked in cold water.)

After soaking, discard the water and boil the legumes in enough water to cover. Any remaining cooking water can be used in soups, sauces, or to thin legume purées. It is not necessary to soak lentils before cooking.

Indian Red Lentil Curry (Dhal)

※

This is our favorite legume recipe. Devanando had this dish on his trip to Pakistan, India, and Ceylon, and he fell in love with it. In some countries red lentils are the most prestigious of all legumes because not everyone can afford them.

※

1 cup red lentils

2 cups water

1 tsp. granulated vegetable bouillon

½ tsp. turmeric powder

1 large onion, cut in half and sliced

¼ cup clarified butter (see Uncommon Ingredients for preparation)

2 tbs. fresh ginger, cut into thin strips

1 chili pepper, minced, with or without seeds (optional)

½ tsp. cumin, ground

½ tsp. coriander, ground

½ tsp. cardamom powder

1 tsp. crumbled curry leaves

¼ tsp. asafetida (optional)

2 tomatoes, diced

Herb salt, to taste

¼ bunch fresh coriander or lovage, chopped

Red lentils do not need to be soaked. Cooked for 15 to 20 minutes they are relatively easy to digest, especially if you add the spices we suggest in this recipe. Spices improve the digestibility of legumes considerably.

In some languages, red lentils are known as "fire lentils." Don't worry, the name comes from their red color, not because they are very spicy. Cooked, they are almost yellow.

In Rajasthan, the Indian desert state with picturesque castles and temples, those who can afford it add huge amounts of clarified butter to their red lentils. Of course, this is not healthful.

Here's our recipe:

Wash lentils and boil them in water with granulated vegetable bouillon, turmeric, and cardamom powder. If water evaporates too quickly, add more. You are trying to get a fairly runny purée. Lentils take approximately 20 minutes to soften.

In the meantime, brown onion rings in clarified butter, which intensifies the flavor of the onions. Add ginger and chili pepper, and sauté 1 to 2 minutes longer. Then add the dry spices.

Stirring constantly, sauté the onion mixture over medium heat for another minute or two. Sautéeing the spices draws out their aromatic oils and intensifies the flavor.

Stir the mixture into the lentils, add the tomatoes, and let stand in a covered pot for 5 minutes. Season with salt. Place in a serving dish and decorate with fresh coriander.

Serve with braised vegetables or rice, millet or unleavened flatbread.

In India this dish is called simply dhal (legumes). You can use other lentils, peas, and even beans to make dhal. Use your imagination when it comes to seasonings. The sky's the limit. Experiment!

Of course you can also restrict yourself to ready-made curry powder, salt, and pepper. If you've never tasted a real Indian dhal, you won't miss the flavor, and you'll still greatly enjoy this dish.

Japanese Beans, Edible Seaweed,
and
Vegetables

❧

Inspired by Japanese culinary art, this dish is very popular at Gourmet's Garden. We like to serve it in the fall and winter.

❧

½ lb. or 1 cup small black beans

2 cups water

3 medium-size onions, diced

½ cup sesame oil

1 clove garlic, crushed (optional)

2 tbs. fresh ginger, cut into small strips

½ tsp. whole cumin

Tamari, to taste

Freshly ground pepper, to taste

1 tsp. granulated vegetable bouillon, dissolved in ½ cup cooking water from the beans

1 oz. edible Hiziki seaweed, soaked in water, cooked until soft, and browned briefly in oil

Lemon juice, to taste

2 large carrots, cut into thin julienne strips

2 leeks, sliced diagonally

¼ lb. or 1 cup fresh shiitake mushrooms, sliced

½ cup rice wine or dry sherry

A small amount of horseradish, freshly ground (or preserved)

Chives, thinly sliced

Soak beans overnight and then simmer until soft. In the meantime, sauté onions using ¼ cup sesame oil, and add garlic, ginger, cumin, and the cooked beans. (Do not add the cooking water, but save it.)

Stirring frequently, sauté the mixture for 5 minutes, and season with tamari and pepper.

Finally, add about ½ cup cooking water from the beans with the vegetable bouillon and the edible seaweed. Season with tamari and lemon juice, and set the dish aside.

Using ¼ cup sesame oil, sauté the vegetables and mushrooms for several minutes in a wok. Add rice wine, cover, and simmer until done. Season with tamari.

Place vegetables in a serving dish, decorate with horseradish and chives, and serve with black beans.

Frijoles Refritos

(Mexican Refried Beans)

❧

This is a national dish of Mexico, and probably the most well known.
Beans are an essential part of most Mexican meals, and the
combination of wheat or corn tortillas and beans is the basic diet
at every level of society. Serve refried beans with tortilla chips,
salsa (see page 189) and guacamole (see page 83).
This makes a marvelous party snack!

❧

½ lb. or 1 cup red kidney beans

3 bay leaves

2 medium-size onions, diced

¼ cup vegetable oil

1 chili pepper, minced (optional)

1 clove garlic, crushed (optional)

⅓ tsp. ground cumin

1 tsp. granulated vegetable
bouillon

Herb salt, to taste

Freshly ground pepper, to taste

Soak beans overnight. Then simmer with bay leaves until soft. When
the beans are done, remove the bay leaves.

Brown onions in a large skillet in vegetable oil. Add chili pepper, garlic,
and cumin. Fry 2 more minutes, stirring constantly. Add the beans without the cooking water, but save the water. Mash the beans using a potato
masher, and add enough of the saved cooking water to make a purée.
Add bouillon, then season with salt and pepper.

If you are serving beans as the main dish, serve with a large, colorful
salad of leaf lettuce, cucumbers, tomatoes, bell peppers, and corn.

SPANISH CHICKPEAS

❦

Why are they called chickpeas? Listen to the sound on the surface
of the water in a bowl of chickpeas you've just put in to soak,
and you'll find out.

❦

1 cup chickpeas

¼ tsp. baking soda (optional)

2 medium onions, minced

¼ cup olive oil

1 yellow bell pepper, diced

1 green bell pepper, diced

6 tomatoes, diced

½ bunch parsley, minced

⅓ cup green olives,
pitted and minced

1 clove garlic, crushed (optional)

Freshly ground pepper, to taste

Herb salt, to taste

Two or three days before you want to prepare this dish, soak the chickpeas in water with baking soda (optional) overnight. Discard the soaking water in the morning. Rinse chickpeas well and let them sprout. (Do not add water.) Rinse three or four times a day, and be especially thorough in warm weather.

After two or three days sprouts will appear, and the chickpeas will be ready to eat. If you don't want to wait that long, soak the chickpeas, and then boil them until they are soft. Of course, the sprouts are better for you.

Sauté onion in olive oil, and add bell peppers. When they are tender, add tomatoes and chickpea sprouts or cooked chickpeas. Season with remaining ingredients.

This dish is particularly good cold as an appetizer. It also makes a good hot main course. Serve with buttered whole grain baguettes.

Exotic Lentils
with
Vegetables and Coconut Sauce

❧

This is not the classic lentil and sausage soup your mother
used to make, but our own, new creation.
Lentils, by the way, sprout very easily.

❧

¼ lb. or ½ cup lentils

1 ¼ cup white wine

3 bay leaves

1 tsp. granulated vegetable
bouillon

2 onions, minced

¼ cup vegetable oil

2 red bell peppers

2 leeks

2 bananas (not too soft)

1 cup grated coconut

❧

SAUCE:

¾ cup water

5 oz. coconut cream
(thickened coconut milk)

1–2 tsp. curry powder

Herb salt, to taste

Freshly ground pepper,
to taste

Simmer lentils, white wine, bay leaves, and vegetable bouillon over low
heat until done.

Meanwhile, sauté onions in oil. Add bell peppers and leeks. Cover and
braise over low heat until everything is as soft as you like it.

When ready, add sliced bananas, and remove from heat.

Mix all the vegetables together and place in a serving bowl. Garnish with coconut shavings.

To prepare the sauce, boil water, dissolve the coconut cream, and season with curry, salt, and pepper.

This is a complete meal. Offer a side dish of grain only if you have very hungry mouths to feed.

TOFU AND TOFU MEXICANA

≈

Tofu, a soybean product, originally came to us from China and Japan. Now it is produced in the West as well. Tofu is, so to speak, a soy cheese, made of soy milk. It contains water, up to 8% protein, 4% fat, and about 3% carbohydrates as well as a variety of minerals, including calcium. People who have become vegetarians are particularly fond of tofu, since it is high in protein. Tofu has next to no taste of its own, and its texture is not particularly appealing. Tofu only becomes interesting after it has been marinated, seasoned, sautéed, deep-fried, baked, or frozen, and then cooked, which gives it a firmer texture. Here is one tofu recipe we want to share with you because it has been very popular at Gourmet's Garden for years.

≈

½ lb. or 1 cup tofu, diced into ½ inch pieces

10 green stuffed olives, pitted and minced

3 tbs. olive oil

2 tomatoes, diced

Juice of 2 limes or 1 large lemon

1 small red onion, finely diced

1 chili pepper, minced

Herb salt, to taste

½ bunch fresh coriander leaves (cilantro)

Freshly ground pepper, to taste

Mix all ingredients and season with salt and pepper. Let stand in a cool place for one hour.

If you are cooking any of the vegetable dishes in this book, you can always add a few diced pieces of tofu.

If you are going to sauté the tofu in a skillet, marinate it in tamari and spices for a while before cooking. If you like it chewy, freeze marinated tofu for several hours, and then let it thaw.

Tempeh Variations

Tempeh comes from Indonesia. It is a fermented soybean product,
available in health food stores. It contains about 20% protein
(like meat) and has a more interesting flavor than tofu—though only
if it is properly prepared and seasoned. It comes in ⅜ –1¼ inch slices
in which you can see individual beans (cooked), and the mushroom
mycelium, similar to Camembert cheese. Here are three ways
to prepare tempeh. All call for cooking with heat.

1. Cut tempeh into ⅛ inch strips and sauté or deep fry. Season with
    herb salt and pepper, and serve either as a side dish or a main dish
    with stir-fried Chinese vegetables or tahini (see pages 20 and 33).

2. Bread a thin tempeh slice like a cutlet, using beaten egg, pepper,
    herb salt, and bread crumbs. Sauté in a skillet. Serve with braised
    vegetables.

3. Add diced tempeh to any dish with a sauce. Let it simmer for a few
    minutes. It will soften and some people like it best that way.

Please note:
Tofu, tempeh, seitan and commercial soy products such as soy sausages,
textured soy protein, TVP (textured vegetable protein), soy granules, soy
mixes for veggie burgers, and similar products can be used as substitutes
for meat and may make life easier during the transition period from
becoming a meat-eater to becoming a vegetarian. But we do not recommend these foods for the long run because they are not highly nutritious.
The protein is denatured, and many of these products go through a long
production process with the inherent disadvantages. These foods may
satisfy old cravings and certainly are better for you than meat, but they
stress the body more than they help it. This is partly due to the fact that
to achieve a flavor similar to meat, they have to be breaded, sautéed, or
deep-fried, none of which is healthful or recommended.

VEGETARIAN PATTIES

and

BURGERS

Hearty Veggie Burgers

¼ lb. or ½ cup carrots,
finely grated

¼ lb. or ¾ cup leeks,
thinly sliced

½ bunch parsley, minced

1 clove garlic, crushed
(optional)

1 peperoncini or chili pepper
with or without seeds (optional)

¼ lb. or ½ cup celery root,
thinly grated

7 oz. tofu,
finely mashed with a fork

1 small red onion, minced

¼ inch ginger root, grated

1 tsp. granulated vegetable
bouillon

Herb salt, to taste

Freshly ground pepper,
to taste

Knead all ingredients together, season with salt and pepper, and shape 10 small burgers or 6 larger burgers.

Bake on a greased baking sheet at 375° F.

TURKISH LENTIL BALLS

⚘

This dish comes from Turkey. Its taste is a real surprise and exactly
what you need to encourage you to give up eating meat.
You'll notice again the importance of spices.
Even meat, as everyone knows, tastes dull without seasoning.

⚘

½ lb., 8 oz., or 1 cup red
lentils

¼ lb. or ½ cup bulgur

1 medium onion, minced

½ lb. or ½ cup bulgur

¼ cup sesame oil

½ tsp. ground cumin

½ tsp. ground coriander

1 clove garlic, crushed

2 tsp. granulated
vegetable bouillon

Freshly ground pepper, to taste

Herb salt, to taste

Boil lentils and bulgur separately. Brown onions in sesame oil.

Add spices, garlic, and vegetable bouillon, and sauté another minute.
Place all the ingredients in a bowl and knead them. Season with salt and
pepper and shape little balls, which you can eat as they are.

They can also be placed on a baking sheet in the oven or warmed in a
sauce (see pages 67–70). They go well with braised vegetables or grains.

FALAFEL

❧

Falafel are little chickpea balls very popular in the Middle East.
They are usually served with hummus (see page 155) and unleavened
bread (pita bread). For a Middle Eastern feast, prepare these three
dishes: falafel, tabbouleh (see page 111), and baba ghanouj
(see page 159). Serve with a large colorful salad with lots of herbs.

❧

For the falafel, you will need:

½ lb., 8 oz., or 1 ½ cups
chickpeas

½ tsp. baking soda,
(for soaking chickpeas)

¼ lb. or ½ cup bulgur

1–2 cloves garlic, crushed

3 scallions, minced

¼ cup sesame seeds

½ tsp. ground cumin

½ tsp. ground coriander

1 tbs. minced parsley

1 tsp. baking powder or baking
soda (for falafel mixture)

Salt, to taste

Freshly ground pepper, to taste

Soak the chickpeas with ½ teaspoon of baking soda overnight. Rinse
well and grind them very, very finely.

Next, cover bulgur with boiling water and let stand for 10 minutes.
Then squeeze out the water. Blend all the ingredients and place the
mixture in the refrigerator for one hour.

With wet hands, shape flat patties of approximately 2 tablespoons of
the mixture. Then place patties on a greased baking sheet and bake in a
375° F oven for about 30 minutes. Of course, you can also fry it, as it is
done in the Middle East. For health reasons, we do not recommend frying.

In the Middle East falafel are rolled up in unleavened bread (pita bread)
with hummus and herbs.

SOUPS

Soups

❧

At the court of Louis XIV several chefs were kept exclusively to prepare soup. Napoleon, who was both gourmet and gourmand, is said to have complained to his chef about the bad soup while in exile on St. Helena. Brillat-Savarin wrote in his remarkable book, *The Physiology of Taste*, "Soup is a healthy, light, nourishing food, good for everyone. It pleases the stomach, prepares it to digest more food, and stimulates the appetite." He praised soup as "the foundation of French nutrition." Of course, in his day, meat stock served as the basis for most soups, though purely vegetarian recipes based on potatoes, grain, or vegetables (Italian minestrone, for example) were also eaten.

We distinguish between two kinds of soup. The first five soups are prepared with raw foods. Eat them at room temperature or heat them slightly in a steamer. They are particularly suitable for the summer. The rest of the soups are what we call "real" soups. On a cold morning or during the winter you will want them simply because they warm the body.

CREAMED RAW VEGETABLE SOUP

2 cups freshly extracted
carrot juice

2 tomatoes, diced

1 ripe (soft) avocado, peeled

1 small red onion, minced
(optional)

1 bell pepper, diced

1 small cucumber, diced

½ bunch parsley, minced

Freshly ground pepper, to taste

Herb salt, to taste

Purée all ingredients, and season with pepper and salt. The avocado
makes the soup creamy.

CREAMED RAW TOMATO SOUP

3 large beefsteak tomatoes

1 cup almond milk, celery
juice, or water

1 ripe (soft) avocado,
peeled and pitted

1 tsp. lemon juice

1 tsp. curry powder

Oregano, to taste

Basil, to taste

Ground cumin, to taste

Freshly ground pepper, to taste

Herb salt, to taste

Purée all ingredients and season with curry, oregano, basil, cumin, salt,
and pepper.

CREAMED RAW CARROT SOUP

⚜

3 cups freshly extracted
carrot juice

1 soft ripe avocado,
peeled and pitted

½ cup cashew nuts,
soaked for a few hours or
overnight

1–2 tsp. ground cumin,
to taste

Freshly ground pepper,
to taste

Herb salt, to taste

Purée the first three ingredients, and season with cumin, salt and pepper

CREAMED RAW FENNEL AND CELERY SOUP

⚜

¾ cup juice of celery root
or green celery

2½ cups freshly extracted
fennel juice

1 soft ripe avocado,
peeled and pitted

½ cup sunflower seeds,
soaked overnight

1 tbs. lemon juice

Freshly ground pepper, to taste

Herb salt, to taste

Purée the first four ingredients in a food processor, and season with
lemon juice, salt, and pepper.

Avocado Soup
from
Kerala (India)

❧

This soup comes from Kerala, a gorgeous area of lagoons and palms in southern India. Devanando thinks of it as the most blessed place on earth. Its opulent beauty, natural abundance, and bustling population combine to create an unforgettable experience.

❧

2 cups water

1 soft, ripe avocado, peeled and pitted

1 ½ cups shredded coconut

½ cup plain yogurt

1 chili pepper, minced with or without seeds (depending on how hot you like it)

½ tsp. ground cumin

2 tbs. lemon juice

1 clove garlic, crushed (optional)

Herb salt, to taste

Freshly ground pepper, to taste

2 tbs. minced fresh coriander leaves (cilantro) for garnish

Purée all ingredients and season with salt and pepper. Garnish each portion with coriander and serve immediately.

Delicious Vegetable Soup

≈

This vegetable soup is not boiled, but simply left to steep.
It's easy to prepare and the varieties are endless.

≈

For three people, bring 2 to 4 cups of water to a boil and add a variety of chopped vegetables. Root vegetables are a particularly good choice because of their pungent flavor.

Reduce the heat to very low immediately after the vegetables are added. This soup should not boil. After 5 minutes remove the pot entirely from the heat.

Let it stand, covered, until the vegetables have reached the desired softness (10 to 30 minutes).

Season with granulated vegetable bouillon, or soy sauce, lemon juice and/or pepper, and herb salt, or any herbs of your choice, perhaps a little bit of freshly ground ginger.

When the soup is ready to be served, sprinkle it generously with whatever chopped, fresh herbs you prefer. Of course, you can also enrich the soup with butter or vegetable oil.

To make a vegetable broth, chop the vegetables into very small pieces, and let the soup stand for a while before you strain it.

For a cream of vegetable soup, purée the steeped vegetables with part of the broth. Let it steep a little longer, and enrich with a little cream.

For more flavor, or if you have invited gourmets to dinner, serve your soup with one teaspoon of basil butter per person (see page 161) or a little grated cheese.

INDIAN LENTIL SOUP
with
SPROUTS

Prepare Indian Red Lentil Curry, or Dhal (see pages 121–122). Finely chop the tomatoes called for in this recipe.

Add water or granulated vegetable bouillon until the soup has the consistency you desire. Season with herbs listed in the recipe.

Then add a handful of lentil sprouts to each serving and garnish with fresh minced coriander or lovage.

KICHADIE

A variation on Indian Lentil Soup with Sprouts is Kichadie, a favorite soup in the Ayurvedic kitchen. It calls for rice and 1½ times as much red lentils, cooked with plenty of water.

In India this is considered the ideal food for people who suffer from chronic diarrhea, ulcers, or poor digestion, and for those who want a light diet. It is the kind of gentle food that is frequently seasoned only with salt, but still tastes wonderful.

If you are well, you can season your kichadie like lentil soup (see above) or use your imagination. Several kinds of vegetables can be cooked along with the lentils.

Miso Soup

❧

Miso is a soft, dark purée, made of fermented soybeans, barley
or rice, and sea salt. It is stored and left for months or years to ripen.
Miso is slightly sweet and very delicate, and is used to season
soups and sauces. For a simple miso soup breakfast,
add one teaspoon of miso to a large glass of warm water.
If you want a real soup, follow this recipe:

❧

3 cups water

*About 2 ½ inches Wakame
seaweed, soaked for
5 minutes, rinsed and cut
into 9 pieces*

1 leek, thinly sliced

*½ inch fresh ginger root,
slivered*

3 tbs. miso

Tamari, to taste

Soy sauce, to taste

*Chopped green onions,
chives, or herbs, to taste*

Bring water to a boil, and add seaweed and leek. Simmer over low heat
for about 5 minutes. Add ginger and wait until the soup is cool enough
to eat.

Pour a few tablespoons of the soup in a cup, stir in miso, and pour it back
into the soup. This way heat does not destroy the enzymes in the miso.
Season with tamari or soy sauce, and sprinkle each portion with
chopped greens.

This basic soup can, of course, be varied according to taste. You could
use different edible seaweed or try sea vegetables, dulse, or hiziki. Or
place a handful of sprouts in each plate, and pour the soup over them.

Chopped mushrooms, such as Shiitake, go very well with miso. One dried and soaked mushroom is enough for three people, since the flavor is very strong. Or try button mushrooms or different chopped vegetables. Celery root is also good with miso. Be creative!

Miso contains live enzymes, which are believed to strengthen the blood, stimulate digestion, and supply the body with other necessary substances. Legend has it that miso was a gift of the gods to humankind, meant to ensure health, happiness, and longevity. Medical studies in Japan have shown that people who eat miso soup daily have a lower than average rate of cancer, heart disease, and other illnesses.

When you buy miso, make sure it is natural, free of chemicals and not a canned (highly heated) product. There are many kinds of miso; get advice from your local oriental market or health food store if you plan to become a miso soup aficionado.

CREAMED CARROT SOUP
with
CORIANDER

3 cups water

1 tbs. granulated vegetable bouillon

1 large onion, minced

8 medium carrots, coarsely grated

Grated peel of ¼ lemon

Juice of ½ lemon

2 tsp. coriander seed, freshly grated

Herb salt, to taste

Freshly ground pepper, to taste

4 tbs. sour cream

2 tbs. chopped parsley

In a covered pot, heat water with bouillon, onion, and carrots. Simmer over low heat until carrots and onions are soft.

Purée the vegetables. Season with the next five ingredients, and divide into individual portions.

Garnish each plate with a dollop of sour cream and some parsley.

Thai Vegetable Soup
with
Lemon Grass

❧

The Thai people love soup. Many families start the day with a light soup, generally a broth with meat, fish, vegetables and/or noodles. They season their soups with lemon grass, fresh ginger and, as in the following example, coconut cream. This soup is very satisfying and supplies the body with warmth, which makes it especially suitable for people who often feel cold.

❧

3 cups water

1 tbs. minced basil

1 tbs. granulated vegetable bouillon (or more to taste)

4 stalks lemon grass, sliced diagonally

1 tbs. fresh lemon leaves cut into very thin strips

1 tbs. fresh ginger root, slivered

3 oz. thickened coconut milk (coconut cream)

Herb salt, to taste

Freshly ground pepper, to taste

1 tsp. lime or lemon juice

½ lb. or 2 cups thinly sliced Chinese cabbage

½ cup lentil or mung bean sprouts

1 scallion, thinly sliced

½ cup green peas, fresh or frozen

Slowly bring water and the next five ingredients to a boil. Let steep over low heat for 15 minutes. Remove lemon grass and discard.

Add coconut cream, and season with salt, pepper, and lime or lemon juice.

Add remaining ingredients, and let soup steep briefly. Serve immediately.

CHINESE VEGETABLE SOUP
with
SHERRY

❦

3 cups water

1 tbs. granulated
vegetable bouillon

½ cup soy sauce

1 cup rice wine or dry
white wine (optional)

3 bay leaves

¼ lb. or ¾ cup leeks,
sliced diagonally

¼ lb. or 1 cup button
mushrooms, sliced

¼ cup sesame oil

½ cup mung bean sprouts

4 tbs. dry sherry

Fresh herbs for garnish

Bring water and the first four ingredients to a boil, then let it stand, covered, for 20 minutes over the lowest possible heat.

In the meantime, sauté leek and mushrooms in sesame oil until they are soft. Add to the soup and season.

To serve, put the bean sprouts and sherry into individual bowls, and then fill them up with the soup. Garnish with a few fresh herbs.

Our Potato Soup

꽃

We could not get along without this old favorite. We all love potato soup because it reminds us of our childhood. You'll have to find out for yourselves whether our recipe is the kind you like best.
If not, you'll soon figure out what to change.

꽃

*4 medium potatoes,
scrubbed and diced
(peeled, if they are old)*

*3 leeks (white part only),
thinly sliced*

3 cups water

2 large onions

*2 tbs. clarified butter
(see Uncommon Ingredients
for preparation)*

1 tbs. olive oil

½ cup cream

*2 tsp. granulated vegetable
bouillon*

*Freshly ground pepper,
to taste*

Herb salt, to taste

*2 tsp. minced fresh chervil
or parsley*

Boil potatoes and leeks in water until soft. In the meantime, brown onions in clarified butter and olive oil. Stir frequently.

Pass potatoes and leeks through a food mill, and return the potato-leek mixture to the soup pot. You can also use a potato masher, but you won't get a smooth consistency. We don't recommend using an electric beater or a blender; they make the potatoes gummy.

Add sautéed onions, cream, and granulated vegetable bouillon, along with some pepper. Season with salt. Garnish each portion with minced chervil or parsley.

Indian Tomato Soup with Cumin

1 medium onion, minced

1 green bell pepper,
cut into julienne strips

1 tbs. cumin, freshly ground

¼ cup sesame oil or clarified
butter (see Uncommon
Ingredients for preparation)

6 tomatoes, skinned and diced

3 cups water

8 oz. or 1 cup red lentils,
rinsed in warm water

1 tbs. granulated vegetable
bouillon

Herb salt, to taste

Freshly ground pepper, to taste

2 tbs. fresh coriander leaves
(cilantro), lovage, or parsley

Brown onions, bell pepper, and cumin for several minutes in oil or clarified butter. Add the next four ingredients, and simmer until lentils are soft and falling apart. Season with pepper and salt.

Garnish individual portions with cilantro, lovage, or parsley.

PURÉES

and

VEGETARIAN PÂTÉS

Purées and
Vegetarian Pâtés

᷉

In this section, we recommend our favorite purées, which you can eat alone or with other dishes, and you can spread on bread. Purées are very popular, perhaps because they remind us of the mashed baby food on which we were all raised, the first nourishment after mother's milk. Mashed foods are often tied to feelings of security and mother love. This probably explains why we long for puréed, creamy foods when we don't feel well and when we are lonely and need consolation. If you are feeling down, try something from this section.

Delicate Fresh Fruit Purées

For a good fruit purée, mash a variety of fruits, if possible using a Champion juicer. (Instead of using the sieve, simply close the lid.)

Add bananas for a creamy consistency. Avoid too many watery fruits like melon. And when you do choose to eat melon, always eat it by itself to derive the full benefits. Here are some good combinations:

- Peaches (or apricots), mangos (or papayas or pears), and bananas
- Apples, pineapples (or carrots), and bananas
- Papayas, soaked dates, and bananas

If the flavor of the fruit is not enough, season your purée with freshly grated ginger, cinnamon, cardamom, or fresh herbs. Use your imagination.

Munich-Style Bean Sprout Pâté

1 ½ cups or 8 oz. mung bean or lentil sprouts	¼ garlic clove, crushed
1 medium tomato	1 tbs. fresh savory or lovage, minced
½ bell pepper	Herb salt, to taste
2 tbs. red onion, minced	Freshly ground pepper, to taste

Purée all ingredients and season with salt and pepper. Adjust consistency by adding another tomato or water.

This is good with vegetables, salad, or bread.

Hummus

❧

Hummus is very popular in the Middle East,
where it is made with cooked chickpeas.

❧

1 ½ cups chickpea sprouts or
boiled chickpeas

3 oz. tahini (sesame purée)

¼ cup sesame oil

¼ cup lemon juice

½ – 1 cup water (depending on
desired consistency)

1 clove garlic, crushed

1 tbs. parsley, minced

Herb salt, to taste

Freshly ground pepper, to taste

Purée all ingredients, and season with salt and pepper.

Hummus is very good with bread or falafel (see page 134) and salad.

Mediterranean Olive and Pepper Pâté

❧

You'll love this if you're fond of hearty food.

❧

1 bell pepper, diced

1 cup black olives, pitted

¼ cup olive oil

1 tbs. lemon juice

1 tbs. fresh basil, minced

Freshly ground pepper, to taste

Purée all ingredients. If you want the pâté especially creamy, substitute 7 ounces. of mascarpone for the oil.

Bettina's Avocado Purée

❧

2 soft, ripe avocados

1 tbs. lemon juice, freshly squeezed

½ tsp. fresh ginger root, grated

½ tsp. cinnamon

1 tsp. honey or 2 tsp. grade C maple syrup

1 cup cream

Mint leaves for garnish

Purée avocados and blend with the next four ingredients. Whip cream until stiff, and fold it into the purée. Garnish individual portions with a mint leaf before serving. This makes a wonderful dessert.

For a quick and easy sandwich spread, mash 2 ripe avocados with a fork and season with a little garlic, lemon juice, minced herbs of your choice, salt, and pepper. This is similar to guacamole (see page 83), which is another kind of avocado purée.

For breakfast, Brazilians purée one ripe avocado per person with the juice of a large orange. This frothy drink is served dusted with cinnamon and is called Vitaminada.

SAVORY NUT PÂTÉ

1 ½ cups sunflower seeds

1 cup almonds or cashews

¼ cup sesame seeds

1 large beefsteak tomato

1 tbs. parsley

Freshly ground pepper, to taste

Herb salt, to taste

Soak sunflower seeds, almonds, and sesame seeds overnight in water. Rinse well and let the damp seeds stand a few hours more. Skin the almonds if you wish.

Purée all ingredients, and season with salt and pepper.

If you prefer to shorten preparation time, use preserved nut purée.

The first three ingredients alone, puréed with a little water, make a good paste. You can vary the seasonings.

Bean Pâté Provençal

꙰

Was there ever a time when you liked liverwurst? Do you still like it?
If so, this recipe is for you. Again you will see that taste depends
primarily on seasonings and consistency. Animal products
are not necessary.

꙰

½ cup red kidney beans	½ tsp. marjoram
1 onion, minced	¼ tsp. herbes de provence
1 leek, thinly sliced	¼ tsp. savory
¼ cup sunflower oil	Approximately ¼ cup water
½ clove garlic, crushed	Herb salt, to taste
2 tbs. black Indian mustard seeds (optional)	Pepper, to taste

Soak beans overnight, and discard soaking water in the morning. Then
boil the beans in plenty of water until soft. Let cool.

In the meantime, brown the onion and leek in oil until they are soft and
the onion has turned brown. Add garlic and mustard seeds (optional),
and sauté one minute longer.

Finally, add the seasonings and purée all the ingredients. Adjust the
amount of water so that you get a solid paste.

This bean pâté is an excellent sandwich spread. It keeps for several days
refrigerated and even longer in a covered jar. Surprise your guests with
snacks made of slices of a whole-grain baguette, bean pâté and a slice of
dill pickle.

Vegetable Purée Variations

🍃

Here are a few simple vegetable purées that you will enjoy.

🍃

Purée cooked carrots or put them through a meat grinder. Cover braised zucchini slices or braised broccoli florets with this carrot paste and herbs—a pleasure for eyes and taste buds.

If you prefer something more substantial, add granulated vegetable bouillon, pepper, salt, chopped herbs, curry, and whatever you like to the carrots.

Parsnips, parsley roots, celery root, and (cooked) eggplant are also all suitable for puréeing, though you'll have to make do without the lovely color of carrots. Enrich the purées with olive oil, cream, or mascarpone.

In the Middle East, a popular eggplant purée made with olive oil, chopped chili pepper, garlic, lemon juice, herb salt, and pepper is called baba ghanouj. A popular variation is made with olive oil, garlic, lots of dill, pepper, herb salt, diced goat cheese, and chopped walnuts. This culinary delight is an indispensable part of every Middle Eastern buffet (see page 134).

CREAMY POTATO PURÉE

1 lb. potatoes boiled in the skin, then peeled

¾ cup cream

1 tsp. granulated vegetable bouillon

Herb salt, to taste

Freshly ground pepper, to taste

Water as needed

Mash the potatoes in a vegetable mill or with a potato masher. Mix in all other ingredients. Use water to adjust the consistency. Season with salt and pepper. You may substitute butter and water for the cream.

If you do not use dairy products you can prepare your beloved mashed potatoes with water and vegetable oil. Experiment until you find the oil you like best.

In Greece they make a special, cold variation of mashed potatoes. Mix 2 parts mashed potatoes with 1 part ground walnuts. Add olive oil and water, and season with garlic, lemon juice, minced parsley, pepper, and salt. This is called skordalia and is a very popular appetizer.

Our reasons for including a recipe for mashed potatoes are twofold: 1) We are very fond of them ourselves, and 2) as nutritional consultants we have noticed over the years that potatoes are actually therapeutic for many of our clients. We can cite examples of people who had completely made the transition to a raw food diet, and suddenly ate nothing but mashed potatoes for weeks on end, greatly improving their spirits. Eventually, the craving for potatoes vanished as suddenly as it came. How senseless it would have been to fight it.

Herb Butter

Seasoning butter with herbs is a nice touch, especially for guests. You can use a variety of herbs, for example, basil, sage, and lovage. Garlic is also very good. We recommend 3 tablespoons chopped herbs or a crushed garlic clove and a pinch of salt for 4 ounces of butter.

First purée the herbs and/or garlic in a mortar. Add softened butter and mix thoroughly.

Herb butter is wonderful on a warm whole-grain baguette. This is especially delicious when the bread is sliced lengthwise, brushed with the butter mixture, put back together, and baked until crisp.

BEVERAGES

Beverages

W ITHOUT A DOUBT, the best beverage is clean water, as low in minerals as possible. You can always depend on water to quench your
thirst, and water plays a considerable part in the internal cleansing of the
body. Water is not the drink of choice, however, for providing your body
with important vitamins, minerals, and trace elements. The minerals
found in water play a minimal role in providing what the body requires.
Use fruits and vegetables instead, especially freshly extracted juices. As
we mentioned earlier, never use ordinary centrifugal electric juicers
because they destroy the curative power of juices. Remember that nothing can replace freshly extracted juice. Forget all those bottled drinks,
even the expensive concoctions sold in health food stores. They have all
been heated, and heat destroys most of the nutrients.

FRESHLY SQUEEZED FRUIT
and
VEGETABLE JUICES

❦

In addition to mono-juices using only one fruit or vegetable,
we recommend the following blends:

apple and green leaf salad juice with herbs

apple and carrot juice

apple and red beet juice

apple, red beet, and cucumber juice

apple, cucumber, celery, and mint juice

apple, peach, and celery juice

apple and pineapple juice

apple, carrot, red beet, and celery juice

carrot and celery or celery root juice

carrot and peach juice

apple, grapefruit, peach, and pear juice

tomato, celery, parsley, and lemon juice with a pinch of pepper

carrot, tomato, and spinach juice

pineapple and orange juice

Nut Milk

❦

Nut milk, especially almond milk, is vastly superior to animal milk,
and it is very easy to prepare.

❦

Soak almonds (or other nuts) overnight in lukewarm water. In the
morning, discard the soaking water, and skin the almonds. Purée 1 part
almonds with 2–4 parts fresh low mineral water in a blender or food
processor with chopping attachment.

If you like, you can put the soaked almonds through a classic little
almond mill before putting it in the blender. Press any remaining pieces
through a fine strainer. If necessary, add a little more water, purée again,
and put the purée through a fine strainer again.

Of course, you can also make nut milk from commercial almond purées
or nut purées by simply adding a little water. This milk is less nutritious,
since the almonds or nuts in commercial purées are usually roasted
before they are ground. Ask if they are pre-roasted before you buy.

❦

Drinks Mixed with Nut Milk

Nut milk makes a delicious drink by itself or mixed with other ingredients. Try, for instance, mixing nut milk with soaked, pitted dates. If you
don't bother to put the milk through a strainer, this takes very little
time.
Simply purée the almonds in water, and add the soaked dates and the
soaking liquid.

This mixture tastes very good by itself, but you can vary the flavor by adding cinnamon, cardamom, natural vanilla, or carob powder. Experiment with other fruits, too. Add a banana for a thicker consistency.

Even though this does not follow the guidelines for harmonious combinations, if you restrict yourself to one glass of any of these drinks, and drink it slowly on an empty stomach several hours before the next meal, you probably won't be bothered by indigestion.

DESSERTS

Desserts

❧

HUMANS, NOT TO MENTION other animals, love sweets. This seems to be an innate craving that is intensified by our environment and certain kinds of behavior. We often associate sweets with love, and sometimes we try to make up for the absence of love by overindulging in sweets. Even strict vegetarians and people on raw food diets find themselves craving sweet foods.

In recognition of this dilemma, and since we are fond of sweets ourselves, we decided to add this section. We fully expect criticism from some zealots, particularly since some of the combinations are not ideal. If you are fairly healthy and don't overeat, you'll be able to cope with imperfect combinations without harming yourself. Don't forget, it's not what you eat occasionally, but what you eat daily that determines your state of health. Remember, too, that troubles with sugar are usually the result of eating sweets on an already full stomach, especially a stomach full of raw food, when the danger of fermentation is particularly great. Socrates was right when he wrote, "A sweet dessert will never hurt you, as long as it is eaten as a meal unto itself."

BLISS BALLS

꙳

Dried fruit alone, or mixed with seeds and nuts, makes marvelous
(and very nourishing) little balls, known to the health food crowd
as "bliss balls." They're ideal for snacks between meals and to
take hiking, mountain climbing, or exercising.

꙳

Here are some basic rules for preparing bliss balls:

1. Always soak seeds and nuts overnight.

2. You can soak dried fruit, but if you do, be careful that the kneaded
   mass of chopped fruit and nuts doesn't get too watery. In other
   words, the amount of dried fruit and the length of time you soak it
   determine the consistency of the fruit balls.

3. If you are working with small quantities, mash the nuts with a pestle first, and then add the dried fruit. Shape little balls and roll
   them in coconut flakes or sesame seeds (unsoaked).

4. You can prepare large quantities very successfully in a Champion
   juicer with the juice spout closed. You can also use a blender or food
   processor with a chopping blade if the mixture is sufficiently
   puréed. In that case, adjust the consistency with the dry ingredients—fine coconut flakes, carob powder, popped amaranth, finely
   chopped dried fruit (unsoaked). Chop fruit and knead it by hand.

5. You can also chop dried fruit finely with a knife, and then knead it
   with the other ingredients.

6. Use a little honey as a sweetener and experiment with various
   spices.

7. Don't make too many bliss balls at once. Wrapped well, they can be kept in the refrigerator, but the flavor fades with time.

The following recipes are combinations we know to be good. The numbers stand for the ratios of amounts used in the recipes.

Fruit Balls

1 part raisins

1 part figs

1 part dates

1 part apricots

Roll in coconut flakes or sesame seeds.

Indian Bliss Balls

1 part dates	*1 part cashews*
	(or hazelnuts)
1 part apricots	*seasoned with cinnamon*
1 part almonds	*and cardamom, or saffron*

Roll in coconut flakes or sesame seeds.

Expand this recipe by adding:
1 part figs, 1 part raisins, 1 part walnuts, 1 part coconut flakes.

Even without spices these little balls are delicious.

SUN BALLS

1 part sunflower seeds

2 parts dates

1 part walnuts

1 part raisins seasoned with cinnamon (optional)

Roll in cocoa or carob powder.

AMARANTH DATE CONFECTION

1 part cashews

1 part dates

1 part popped amaranth seasoned with cardamom

Roll in popped amaranth.

Halvah

1 part sesame purée

1 part almonds

¼ part honey

¼ part carob powder
seasoned with natural vanilla

Roll out ¾ inch thick on a baking sheet or tray.
Let stand in a cool place for a while, and then cut into pieces.

Carob Balls

2 parts almonds

3 parts carob powder

1 part coconut flakes

½ part dates or honey

½ part water (as needed)

Roll in coconut flakes or sesame seeds.

Avocado Dream

4 apples, cored and diced

2 avocados, peeled, pitted, and diced

7 dates, soaked and pitted

About 1 cup water, added gradually

Purée the ingredients. Add water little by little until you reach
the desired consistency. Serve Avocado Dream with Cashew Vanilla or
Banana Cream or Hazelnut Date Cream (see pages 176–178).

Cashew Vanilla Cream

3 bananas, sliced

1 ½ cups cashew nuts, soaked overnight

¼ tsp. natural vanilla

About 1 cup water, added gradually

Purée the ingredients.
Add water little by little until you reach the desired consistency.

Soft Banana Ice with Carob Sauce

Peel ripe bananas (the riper the better because they will be more flavor-ful), and freeze them. Put them through a Champion juicer (with spout closed). You'll get a delicious soft ice which you can eat immediately. If you don't have a juicer, cut the bananas into little pieces before freezing them, and then purée.

To prepare carob sauce, mix 4 ounces tahini (sesame purée) with an equal amount of water, 1 teaspoon honey, and 1 teaspoon carob powder.

Cashew Banana Cream

½ lb. or 2 cups cashew nuts soaked overnight

½ banana (10 slices)

About 7 oz. water

Discard the soaking water. Purée all ingredients.
Add as much water as you like to get to desired consistency.

Hazelnut Date Cream

🌿

½ lb. or 2 cups hazelnuts, soaked overnight

7 dates, soaked for several hours and pitted

About ¾ cup water

Discard the water used for soaking the nuts.
Purée all ingredients with the water used to soak the dates.
Use only enough additional water to get a creamy consistency.

California Dried Fruit Sauce

🌿

1 ½ cups raisins

10 dates, pitted

10 figs, stems removed

1 tsp. tahini

Water

Soak dried fruit for 3–4 hours and purée.
Add tahini and enough water to get the desired consistency.
This sauce goes well with banana ice (see page 177) or fruit salad.

MILLET CREAM
with
HONEY AND FRESH GINGER

½ lb. or 1 cup millet

¼ cup sweet cream

1 tbs. honey

1 tbs. fresh ginger, grated

Cinnamon, to taste

Pour boiling water over the millet either in a sieve or in a pot to get rid of its bitter taste until it is soft and mushy. Then drain all the water. Set aside to cool.

When the millet has cooled, stir in remaining ingredients. Arrange individual portions garnished with fruit soaked in rum or water, or soaked raisins.

KHEERNI

❦

This Indian rice purée from the imperial Mogul kitchens tastes like
something out of *Tales from the Arabian Nights*.

❦

1 cup uncooked or 3 cups cooked Basmati rice

4 ½ cups water

5 oz. coconut cream

2 tbs. honey

2 tbs. rose water

½ tsp. saffron, finely crushed
and dissolved in a small amount of water

½ tsp. cardamom

½ lb. dates, chopped

Simmer rice in water until it is soft and mushy. Make sure there is always
enough water in the pot to keep the rice from burning.

Dissolve coconut cream in the water, and allow it to cool. When it has
cooled, add the next 4 ingredients. Season and serve kheerni on dessert
plates. Garnish with chopped dates.

The Craving for Sweets

To close this section, we want to add a word about craving sweets after meals. Many of us experience these cravings, particularly after a spicy, highly seasoned meal or one with a lot of garlic. You've eaten enough and feel full, but somehow not satisfied. Yet the minute you eat something sweet, you are satiated. We know that sweets after a meal can cause fermentation in the stomach because the sugar cannot leave the stomach quickly enough. This knowledge creates a dilemma. On the one hand, we crave a sweet dessert, on the other, common sense tells us to do without. What's the solution?

You can decrease your intake of spices, particularly garlic. This will decrease your craving for sweets. Or you can give in to your desire for something sweet, and limit the amount of dessert you eat. You needn't consume a mountain of pudding, fruit salad with whipped cream, cake, or chocolate to satisfy your craving. We know from experience that a little bit is enough and will not cause any problems. Even just one or two dates might be sufficient.

HORS D'OEUVRES,

APPETIZERS,

and

SNACKS

Hors d'Oeuvres, Appetizers, and Snacks

⁊

IN THIS FINAL SECTION, we will give you a few more dishes that can be
served as hors d'oeuvres or as part of a cold buffet. We begin with
recipes that complement salads.

Fruit Appetizers

Cut different types of fruit into cubes no larger than ¾ inch, and spear 4 or 5 pieces on a toothpick. Arrange on a tray and serve as guests arrive.

Vegetable Appetizers

Cut a variety of vegetables into slices or cubes, and spear 4 or 5 pieces on a toothpick. Arrange on a tray and garnish attractively.

Tomatoes Filled with Cream

Cut the tops off cherry tomatoes, and hollow them out. Use the tops and insides of the tomatoes to make Avocado Purée (see page ___), and stuff the tomatoes with it.

Stuffed Avocados

Cut ripe avocados in half and remove the pits. Stuff with Ratatouille Salad (see page 41). Make sure you cut the vegetables for the salad into small cubes.

Mushrooms Stuffed with Capers

❧

Use medium-size mushrooms. Remove and chop the stems. Mix with an equal amount of Olive Pepper Pâté (see page 156), without the mascarpone. Garnish each stuffed mushroom with a caper and a mint leaf.

Dream Blossoms

❧

Arrange your party salads on stainless steel serving dishes and garnish generously with edible flowers such as marigolds, nasturtiums, dandelion blossoms, and daisies. Use the leaves and stems as part of the salad or garnish. Your guests will be delighted.

Pinzimonio

❧

Cut carrots, radishes, bell pepper, celery, and similar vegetables into julienne strips. Arrange them upright in shallow goblets or flat, in a circular pattern, on a serving dish.

For dips, try Italian Dressing (see page 30), Gourmet's Dressing (see page 34), and a seed or nut purée dressing (see pages 33–34).

Serve dips in little bowls and dip the vegetable sticks into them. This makes great finger food.

RADISH CARPACCIO

Slice a large radish thinly, and arrange slices in a circular pattern on individual plates. Brighten the picture with slices of small red radishes.

Sprinkle with a small amount of lemon juice and grated Parmesan, pecorino, or a similar cheese. Garnish with fresh basil.

ARUGULA WITH OYSTER MUSHROOMS

Sauté sliced, medium-size oyster mushrooms in olive oil over high heat until they are well-done and slightly crunchy.

Season with a few splashes of lemon juice, herb salt, and freshly ground pepper. Divide into individual portions.

Cover the plates with a bed of arugula, sliced crosswise (or dandelion leaves, spinach, or oak leaf lettuce), and then cover with the browned oyster mushrooms. Garnish with diced tomatoes. Sprinkle with a small amount of Italian Dressing (see page30).

Salsa Mexicana

☙

½ lb. or 1 ¼ cups tomatoes, diced

1 onion, very finely diced

1 clove garlic, crushed

*2 fresh chili peppers with or without seeds
(depending upon how hot you like it), finely minced*

*½ bunch fresh coriander leaves (cilantro) minced,
or fresh parsley, lovage, and other herbs to taste
(nothing can really replace the cilantro in this recipe)*

Juice of 1 lime or ½ lemon

Herb salt, to taste

Freshly ground pepper, to taste

Mix all ingredients and purée ¾ of the mixture. Then add what is left of the mixture. Salsa should be hot and thick, so it is easy to eat with tortilla chips.

This salsa goes well with Refried Beans (see page 125), Guacamole (see page 83), iceberg lettuce cut into small pieces, or sweet corn.

Uncommon Ingredients

🦋

Adzuki bean: A small, dark red bean delicate in texture and slightly sweet. It can be purchased in specialty markets[5] and health food stores.

Arrowroot: A thickener made from a tropical tuber of the same name. It has twice the thickening power of wheat flour, is tasteless, and becomes clear when cooked. Mix with a cold liquid before heating or adding to hot mixtures. Arrowroot can be found in powdered form in supermarkets, health food stores and Asian markets.

Arugula: A leafy salad green shaped like a radish popular in Italy and recently gaining popularity in the United States. To some, arugula tastes a bit bitter. When mixed with milder greens, it can enhance the flavor of salads. It can be found in specialty produce markets or grown from seed. Also called rugula, roquette, rocket, or garden rocket.

Asafetida: Sap from the roots and stem of a giant fennel-like plant found mainly in Iran and India. The sap dries into a hard resin that can be found in lump or ground form in Indian markets. Asafetida has a garlic-

---

5. Specialty markets are privately-owned stores that carry unusual items; every large city has them. Some known nationally are: Frieda's Finest in Los Alamitos, CA (1-800-421-9477); Dean & DeLuca in New York City (1-800-221-7714); Balducci's in New York City; Sutton Place Gourmet in Washington, DC; HayDay in Westport, CT. Many specialize in one kind of ethnic food, such as Italian, Indian, or Asian.

like aroma and should be used sparingly. Excellent in dried beans and vegetables. Can be found in health food stores or Indian markets.

Black Indian mustard seed: Popular in eastern and southern Indian cooking. It is used to flavor chutneys and seafood. When ground, the flavor is pungent and bitter. Can be found in Indian markets and health food stores.

Basmati rice: The "queen" of rice is grown in the foothills of the Himalayas. Aged before it is cooked, the long-grained rice has a perfumy, nutlike flavor and aroma, and because it is very expensive, is only cooked by the very rich of India. It can be found in Indian and Middle Eastern markets and some supermarkets. Basmati rice is also grown in Pakistan and Texas. The latter is sold as Texmati rice. Neither of these variants is as flavorful as authentic Himalayan basmati.

Borage: A coarse plant with dark gray-green hairy leaves and bright flowers that has the scent of cucumber when crushed. Both flowers and leaves can be used in salads but the leaves must be finely chopped to offset their hairy texture. This plant is most often grown for the flower. Sew borage seeds in spring for summer flowering and in autumn for spring flowers. Seeds will drop from the plant and will germinate, coming up again the following year. Fresh borage can be ordered from herb farms (see list of some popular suppliers, on page 199).

Bulgur: Wheat kernels that have been steamed, dried and crushed. The texture is soft and chewy with a nutty flavor. It comes in coarse, medium and fine grinds. Bulgur is a staple of Middle Eastern cooking and is often confused with cracked wheat. It can be found in most supermarkets and health food stores.

Chervil: A member of the parsley family, very mild and faintly sweet in flavor, similar to tarragon. Can be found fresh in most supermarkets and is readily available dried. Chervil can be grown indoors as well as out in the garden. Needs some protection and doesn't tolerate hot weather.

Will self-sew (see Lamb's lettuce) and normally provides one early and one late summer crop.

Chutney: A condiment made from fruit, vinegar, sugar, spices and fresh ginger. A leading brand of Indian-style chutney available in U.S. supermarkets is Major Grey's chutney.

Clarified butter: Also called ghee. Unsalted butter that has been melted down and strained so that the milk solids (and milky residue) are separated from the golden liquid. This golden liquid is the clarified butter. It is very rich and strong in taste and smell, so much less is needed in cooking than fresh butter. Two sticks of butter, or ½ pound, yields about ¾ cup clarified butter.

Cold-pressed oil: Oil made without the use of heat or chemicals.

Curry leaves: Shiny, small leaves from a plant or small tree that grows in tropical and subtropical regions such as India, Sri Lanka and Malaysia. Curry leaves resemble lemon or bay leaves and have a pungent fragrance. Look for bright olive green leaves, with no sign of yellowing or wilting. Refrigerate fresh leaves in an airtight container for up to 2 weeks.

Fresh leaves are preferred, but dried are available and should be bought vacuum-packed. Store in an airtight container after opening. Dried leaves lose flavor and aroma within 1 to 2 months.

Curry leaves are used in Indian and Asian cookery to flavor curries, meat and fish dishes, vegetables, chutneys, pickles and relishes, and as an ingredient in Madras curry mixes. Most Indian markets sell fresh curry leaves. They bear little resemblance to commercial curry powder which is a blend of up to 20 spices.

Dulse: A coarse, red leafy seaweed, dark in color, that is used as a condiment, and found in Iceland, New England and Canada. Available in health food stores.

Fenugreek leaves: An herb that has a taste similar to fresh string beans and can be tossed into a salad. As the plant grows (8 to 10 inches tall), the leaves can be eaten raw, boiled or curried.

Fresh leaves are not readily available in the United States but seeds are available and can be planted in full sun. Small plants can be grown indoors. Dried fenugreek leaves and seeds can be found in most supermarkets and specialty stores.

Galagan: A spice from the Far East with a flavor much like saffron. Used in Indonesian and Thai cooking. Saffron may be substituted for galagan, but it is very expensive so it is used sparingly. Fresh ginger root is also a good substitute, but it does not replace the unique flavor of galagan.

Gomasio: A seasoning made from 9 parts ground sesame seeds and 1 part sea salt.

Herbes de Provence: A mixture of dried herbs commonly found wild or cultivated around Provence, France. Following is a recipe for herbes de Provence:

> *1 tbs. each dried thyme, chervil, tarragon and marjoram*
>
> *1 tsp. each dried oregano, rosemary, summer savory and fennel seed*
>
> *2 Mediterranean bay leaves, crushed*
>
> *Mix thoroughly. Store in an airtight container. Use sparingly.*

Hizihi seaweed: A seaweed used often in soups and added to vegetables and rice. It is said to be high in minerals and vitamins, and is used as a remedy for flatulence. Can be found in oriental markets and health food stores.

Hijiki: Often misspelled in the West as Hiziki. Stringy black sea vegetable sold in lengths of about 1 ½ inches long. It is often used in soups and can be found in health food stores.

Japanese kudzu: A Japanese thickener made from the root of the kudzu vine. In powder form, it can be mixed with water to form a thin paste before being added to another mixture. Available in powder form in Japanese and health food stores. An acceptable substitute is arrowroot.

Kohlrabi: A member of the cabbage family, the edible stem is much like a turnip both in color and taste. Look for kohlrabies heavy for size (under 3 inches in diameter), firm to the touch with dark green leaves.

Young, fresh tender leaves can be sautéed like greens. Trimmed of its leaves, kohlrabi can be stored tightly wrapped for 4 to 5 days in the refrigerator. It is available in supermarkets and green grocers from mid-spring to late fall and is rich in potassium and vitamin C.

Lamb's lettuce: Also known as mache, field salad or corn salad. This plant has dark green leaves that are tender with a buttery, nut-like flavor. The leaves can be used in a salad or steamed and served as a vegetable.

It is a very expensive gourmet green, sometimes found in specialty markets. Seeds can be found in better seed catalogues. It is one of the first plants to come up in spring and will self-sew, which means its seeds will drop off and germinate for the following year.

Lovage: Also known as "false celery" because of its strong resemblance to that plant. Because of its strong celery-like flavor, the leaves, seeds and stalks should be used sparingly to flavor soups, stews and meat dishes.

The seeds, commonly called "celery seed" can be found in supermarkets. Dried lovage leaves and stalks can be found in health food stores and gourmet markets.

Mascarpone: Made in Italy from cow's milk, this is a double-cream to triple-cream cheese. It is excellent with fruit and is used in the Italian dessert, *tiramisu.* Can be purchased in Italian markets, specialty shops and supermarkets.

Mung bean sprouts: Sprouts grown from the mung bean, a small pea-like bean sometimes likened to the soy bean. In its dried form, the bean is ground into flour and used to make noodles in China and India. Sprouted mung beans are available fresh or canned in most supermarkets.

Pecorino cheese: Any cheese made in Italy from sheep's milk. Most of the cheeses are aged and become hard with a sharp flavor. Unaged pecorino is soft, milk-like in flavor and white in color. When aged the color ranges from white to pale yellow. The best known of these is Pecorino Romano. It can be used as you would Parmesan cheese, though Romano has a much sharper flavor. It can be found in Italian markets and some supermarkets.

Peperoncini: Elongated pepper, pickled while green and used in Italian salads. Has a mild flavor and can be found in most supermarkets.

Porcini mushroom: Also known as Cepes, this wild mushroom is pale brown or taupe in color, can weigh from an ounce to a pound and can range in diameter from 1 to 10 inches. Described as having a smoky, woodsy flavor, fresh porcini are seldom found in the United States but you might try Italian or specialty produce markets in late spring and early autumn. Dried are available in Italian specialty markets. Portobello mushrooms may be substituted if absolutely necessary.

Quark: A low-fat curd cheese made in Austria and Germany. It can be purchased in some health food stores and gourmet food stores. An acceptable substitute is whole-milk ricotta or finely curded cottage cheese puréed or sieved with a little sour cream or yogurt added.

Sesame oil and roasted sesame oil: Sesame oil is made from fresh sesame seeds and can be used in large quantities. It is available in most supermarkets.

Roasted sesame oil is made from roasted sesame seeds and has a very strong flavor so it is used in small quantities. It is light brown in color and is sprinkled lightly over many cooked Oriental dishes like a spice. It is available in the oriental foods section of many supermarkets.

Spelt: A coarse European wheat which can be found in health food stores.

Spelt sprouts: Sprouts grown from the spelt seed. This can be done by soaking the seeds in water then placing them in a jar with a lid. Place in a warm environment and wait for them to sprout. Use in salads or on sandwiches. You can find spelt seeds or sprouts at health food stores.

Tahini: A smooth creamy paste made from unroasted (or very lightly roasted), hulled white sesame seeds. Due to the removal of the hulls, tahini is not as nutritious as sesame butter, which is made from whole sesame seeds. Tahini is used in Middle Eastern cooking, especially in making hummus. Can be found in specialty shops and some supermarkets.

Tamari: A dark sauce, thicker than soy, made from soybeans. It has a mild flavor and is used as a condiment, a basting sauce and as a dipping sauce. It can be found in some supermarkets and in oriental markets. Soy sauce can be substituted for tamari.

Tempeh: Made from cooked soy beans cultured with a special bacteria to form a white, distinctively flavored cheese. Often used as a meat substitute because it holds its shape well when cooked, and absorbs other flavors. Tempeh is readily available in health food stores.

Tempeh chips: A cake of cultured soybeans with a flavor and texture similar to southern fried chicken. Best vegetarian source of vitamin B-12.

Wakame seaweed: A nutritious seaweed with long green fronds and a silky texture. It is commonly used in soups and salads.

Before use, soak for 5 minutes and pare away the tough spine. As a soup ingredient it needs very little cooking. To use in salads, scald with boiling water and immediately refresh with cold water. Can be found in Japanese food stores and health food stores.

Following is a list of the better seed companies. They will be useful if you want to grow some of your own ingredients, especially those that are not always readily available.

Burpee and Company
300 Park Avenue
Warminster, PA 18991-001
Phone: (800) 888-1447
Fax: (800) 487-5530

Johnny's Selected Seeds
Foss Hill Road
Albion, Maine 04910-9731
Phone: (207) 437-4301
Fax: (207) 437-2165

Nichols Garden Nursery
1190 North Pacific Highway
Albany, OR 97321-4580
Phone: (541) 928-9280

Seeds Blum
HC 33
Idaho City Stage
Boise, ID 83706
Phone: (800) 742-1423
Fax: (208) 333-5658

Seeds of Change
1364 Rufina Circle #5
Santa Fe, NM 87501
Phone: (505) 438-8080
Fax: (505) 438-7052

Shepherd's Garden Seeds
30 Irene Street
Torrington, CT 06790
Phone: (203) 482-3638
Fax: (203) 482-0532
*Shepherd's also has operators
receiving orders in California.
Their number is:*
Phone: (408) 335-6910
Fax: (408) 335-2080

Smith and Hawken
Two Arbor Lane
P.O. Box 6900
Florence, KY 41022-6900
Orders by Phone:
(800) 776-3336
To order a catalogue:
(800) 981-9888
Order by Fax: (606) 727-1166

**Southern Exposure Seed
Exchange**
P.O. Box 170
Earlysville, VA 22936
Phone: (804) 973-4703
Fax: (804) 973-8717

Territorial Seed Company
P.O. Box 157
Cottage Grove, OR 97424
Phone: (541) 942-9547
Fax: (888) 657-3131

Vermont Bean Seed Company
Garden Lane
Fairhaven, VT 05743
Phone: (802) 273-3400

Following is a list of suppliers of fresh herbs, especially those that might be hard to find.

Creation Gardens
609 East Main Street
Louisville, KY
Phone:(502) 587-9012
(*Also carries almost all varieties
of mushrooms*)

Dean & DeLuca
560 Broadway
New York, NY 10012
Phone: (800) 221-7714
(212) 431-1691

Frieda's Finest
4465 Corporate Center Drive
Los Alamitos, CA 90720
Phone:(800) 421-9744
(714) 826-6100

Herb Time Farms
P.O. Box 2862
So. San Francisco, CA 94083
Phone:(415) 952-4372

Quail Mountain Herbs
P.O. Box 1049
Watsonville, CA 95077-1049
Phone:(408) 722-8456
Fax:(408) 722-9472

Index